A Course in Meditation

A Course in Meditation

A 21-Day Workout for Your Consciousness

OSHO

HARMONY
BOOKS · NEW YORK

This book is compiled from multiple original talks by Osho,
all published in full as books and also available as original audio recordings.
See www.osho.com/library.

Library of Congress Cataloging-in-Publication Data has been applied for.

ISBN 978-1-9848-2596-4
Ebook ISBN 978-1-9848-2597-1

PRINTED IN THE UNITED STATES OF AMERICA

Book design by Andrea Lau
Cover design by Sarah Horgan

First Edition

Contents

A Course in Meditation

INTRODUCTION

If you want to live a more fulfilled life, first you will want to know your potential, who you really are. Meditation is the route to that knowing. It is the methodology of the science of awareness. The beauty of this inner science is that it enables whoever wants to explore and to experiment within, to do so alone. This eliminates dependence on an outer authority, the need to be affiliated with any organization, and the obligation to accept a certain ideology. Once you understand the steps, you walk the walk in your own, individual way.

Many meditative techniques require one to sit still and be silent—which, for most of us with accumulated stress in the body and mind, can be difficult.

But what is meditation exactly? And how can you get started?

This 21-day experiential course is designed to give you a taste of meditation as it is taught by the contemporary mystic Osho. You might already know him from his books, translated and published in more than sixty languages. Osho is a mystic and a scientist, a rebellious spirit whose unique contribution to the understanding of who we are defies categorization. His only interest is to alert humanity to the urgent need to discover a new way of living. Osho's understanding is that only by changing ourselves—one individual at a time—can the outcome of all our "selves"—our societies, our cultures, our beliefs, our world—also change. The doorway to that change is meditation.

For beginning meditators, this is a step-by-step guide to learn meditation, being mindful and still. For experienced meditators, it is the key to taking your practice to a new level. As part of this 21-day program, each day you will be introduced to a different aspect of meditative living, reading (or listening to, through the audiobook) excerpts from Osho's talks as an experience of meditation. Then you will be introduced to simple, practical meditation and awareness exercises related to the subject of the day, as tools to experiment with.

In the suggested reading section at the back of the book, for each day and topic we suggest a book by Osho that goes more deeply into the subject matter addressed in the day's program.

Just as science investigates the outer world, Osho uses a scientific approach to the inner world of meditation and self-discovery. He has experimented with all the meditation techniques developed in the past and has examined their effects on the modern human being. He has seen how difficult it is for the hyperactive 21st-century mind to just sit silently, for example, and watch the breath. Or how easy it is for an ancient sacred mantra to be used just as a replacement for a modern-day sleeping pill. Out of this understanding, he has created new meditations for the people of today. He suggests starting with the body—to become aware of what we can observe in the thoughts and sensations of the body-mind complex. Many of the Osho meditations begin with physical activity to first release the tensions and stress of body and mind. Then, it is easier to relax into an experience of still and silent watchfulness, awareness.

Osho also transformed the "art of listening" into a doorway to meditation. Speaking each day to the people gathered around him—people of all ages, nationalities, and cultural backgrounds—his talks respond to their questions and concerns and lay out his proposal for a saner and more inner-directed way of living. Those talks have been published in the many Osho books now available in the market. Osho emphasized again and again that the talks are not "lectures" to convey information. He says, "My speaking is not oratory; it is not a doctrine that I am preaching to you. It is simply an arbitrary device to give you a taste of what silence is."

In other words, the Osho talks are, in themselves, a meditation. Here, words become music, the listener discovers who is listening, and the awareness moves from what is being heard to the individual doing the hearing.

An audio edition of this guide is also available if you would like to experience Osho's talks as a "listening meditation." Each day you will have the opportunity to hear an original recording, excerpted from an Osho talk that is related to the program of the day. Following the excerpt, you can then also choose to listen to a facilitator who will guide you through each day's meditation technique. Whenever you like, you can come back to the printed text and use the provided pages to create a journal of your experiences.

DAY 1

What Is Meditation?

Today we start with a basic question: *What is meditation?*

Osho's response suggests that meditation is a quality we are born with, and that our task is simply to remember and reconnect with that quality we had as a child.

After each Insight section there will be a meditation and awareness exercise by Osho.

You can experiment with it in your own time, perhaps before you go to sleep tonight.

OSHO'S INSIGHT

Meditation is a state of no-mind. Meditation is a state of pure consciousness with no content. Ordinarily, your consciousness is too much full of rubbish, just like a mirror covered with dust. The mind is a constant traffic: thoughts are moving, desires are moving, memories are moving, ambitions are moving—it is a constant traffic, day in, day out. Even when you are asleep the mind is functioning, it is dreaming. It is still thinking; it is still in worries and anxieties. It is preparing for the next day; an underground preparation is going on.

This is the state of no meditation—just the opposite is meditation. When there is no traffic, and thinking has ceased—no thought moves, no desire stirs, you are utterly silent—that silence is meditation. In that silence truth is known, and never otherwise. Meditation is a state of no-mind. And you cannot find meditation through the mind because mind will perpetuate itself. You can find meditation only by putting the mind aside, by being cool, indifferent, unidentified with the mind; by seeing the mind pass, but not getting identified with it, not thinking that "I am it."

Meditation is the awareness that "I am not the mind."

When the awareness goes deeper and deeper in you, slowly, slowly, a few moments arrive—moments of silence, moments of pure space. Moments of transparency, moments when nothing stirs in you and everything is still. In those still moments you will know who you are, and you will know what the mystery of this existence is.

And once you have tasted those few dewdrops of nectar, great longing will arise in you to go deeper and deeper into it. Irresistible longing will arise in you, a great thirst. You will become afire!

When you have tasted a few moments of silence, of joy, of meditativeness, you will like this state to become your constant state, a continuum. And if a few moments are possible, then there is no problem. Slowly, slowly, more and more moments will be coming. As you become skillful, as you learn the knack of not getting involved in the mind—as you learn the art of remaining aloof, away from the mind, as you learn the science of creating a distance between you and your own thoughts—more and more meditation will be showering on you. And the more it showers, the more it transforms you. A day comes, a day of great blessings, when meditation becomes your natural state.

Mind is something unnatural; it never becomes your natural state. But meditation is a natural state—which we have lost. It is a paradise lost, but the paradise can be regained. Look into the child's eyes, look and you will see tremendous silence, innocence. Each child comes with a meditative state, but he has to be initiated into the ways of the society. He has to be taught how to think, how to calculate, how to reason, how to argue; he has to be taught words, language, concepts. And, slowly, slowly, he loses contact with his own innocence. He becomes contaminated, polluted by the society. He becomes an efficient mechanism; he is no more a man.

All that is needed is to regain that space once more. You had known it before, so when for the first time you know meditation, you will be surprised—because a great feeling will arise in you as if you have known it before. And that feeling is true: you *have* known it before. You have forgotten. The diamond is lost in piles of rubbish. But if you can uncover it, you will find the diamond again—it is yours.

It cannot really be lost, it can only be forgotten.

We are born as meditators, then we learn the ways of the mind. But our real nature remains hidden somewhere deep down like an undercurrent. Any day, a little digging, and you will find the source still flowing, the source of fresh waters. And the greatest joy in life is to find it.

A child is born; the child comes ready with great energy. The child is nothing but pure energy embodied. And the first thing the child has to seek and search for is the mother's breast, obviously. The child is hungry. For nine months in the mother's womb the child was fed automatically; the child lived as part of the mother. Now he is cut from the mother; he has become a separate entity in himself—and the first thing, the first necessity, is to search for food. That's how the outward journey begins.

The entry into the world is through the breast. And the breast did two things: it nourished the child—and the first thing was to survive. And the breast was the food, the breast was life. And the second thing: the breast gave warmth to the child, shelter to the child, love to the child. That's why food and love have become so much associated.

That's why whenever you are not feeling loved, you start

eating too much. The people who become addicted to food are the people who are missing love. They start substituting with food. If you are really loved, you cannot eat too much.

Meditation means becoming aware that the source of life is inside. The body depends on the outside, true—but you are not the body alone. You don't depend on the outside. You depend on the inner world. These are the two directions: to move outwards or to move inwards. Meditation is the recognition that "There is an inner world too, and I have to search for it."

Meditation is mind turning towards its own source.

Mind is a way to understand the object: meditation is a way to understand the subject. Mind is a concern with the contents, and meditation is a concern with the container, the consciousness. Mind becomes obsessed with the clouds, and meditation searches for the sky. Clouds come and go: the sky remains, abides.

Search for the inner sky. And if you have found it, then you will never die.

THE MEDITATION:
EVERYDAY AWARENESS

The following is adapted from *The Book of Secrets* by Osho. It is a simple technique to give you a taste and experience of bringing awareness to activities you do every day. As you experiment with this technique, you can start to reclaim your natural meditative state from all the noise and traffic of the mind.

Osho says:

When I say that awareness cannot be attained by mind, I mean that you cannot attain it by thinking about it. It can be attained only by doing, not by thinking.

*So don't go on thinking about what awareness is, how to achieve it
or what will be the result. Don't go on thinking—start doing it.*

*When walking on the street, walk with awareness. It is difficult, and
you will go on forgetting, but don't be discouraged. Whenever you
remember again, be alert.*

Take every step with full alertness, knowingly.

Remaining with the step, not allowing the mind to move somewhere else.

While eating, eat. Chew your food with awareness.

*Whatever you are doing, don't do it mechanically. For example,
I can move my hand mechanically. But then I can also move my
hand with full alertness. My mind is conscious that my hand is being
moved.*

The Technique

Do it, try it—right now. Reach for an object nearby, and pick it up
as you would normally do, mechanically. Now put it back again.

And now . . . become aware of your hand, feel it from the inside out. If there is any tension in the hand, in the fingers, let the
tension go.

Remaining with the awareness of your hand, with your full
attention on your hand, reach for the object again. Pick it up. Feel
the texture of it, the weight of it. How it feels in your hand. See
how your hand wants to respond to this object . . . to turn it over,
to weigh it, to play with it . . . or simply to hold it still. With alertness, awareness of each movement.

Now put it down, staying alert and aware of the movement of your hand.

You will feel the change. The quality of the action changes immediately.

Osho says:

For example, if you eat with awareness, then you cannot eat more than is needed by the body.

The quality changes. If you eat with awareness, you will chew more. With unconscious, mechanical habits, you simply go on pushing things into your stomach. You are not chewing at all, you are just stuffing yourself. Then there is no pleasure. And because there is no pleasure, you need more food in order to get the pleasure. There is no taste, so you need more food.

Just be alert and see what happens. If you are alert, you will chew more, you will feel the taste more, you will feel the pleasure of eating. And when the body enjoys, it tells you when to stop.

Experiment with this awareness technique today and in the coming days, in different situations—no need to set extra time aside for this meditation. The point is to just meditate, in a relaxed and playful way, while doing these normal, everyday activities. Ordinary things that you normally do without thinking, this time do them in a space of awareness.

Quote of the Day

When mind knows, we call it knowledge.

When heart knows, we call it love.

And when being knows, we call it meditation.

—Osho

Notes

DAY 1 WHAT IS MEDITATION?

DAY 2

Meditations on Love and Relating

It is one thing to bring awareness to our physical actions and the sensations of the body while walking, eating, cleaning the floor, and so on. Or even to become aware of our thoughts and emotions when we are alone, and take a little distance from them. But it's quite another thing to bring that same quality of awareness to our interactions with other people, particularly with our intimate partners. Today's program is about that part of our lives.

OSHO'S INSIGHT

Love is not a relationship. Love relates, but it is not a relationship. A relationship is something finished. A relationship is a noun; the full stop has come, the honeymoon is over. Now there is no joy, no enthusiasm; now all is finished. Relationship means something complete, finished, closed.

Love is never a relationship—love is relating. It is always a river, flowing, unending. Love knows no full stop; the honeymoon begins but never ends. It is not like a novel that starts at a certain point and ends at a certain point; it is an ongoing phenomenon. Lovers end, love continues. It is a continuum. It is a verb, not a noun.

Why do we reduce the beauty of relating to relationship? Why are we in such a hurry?—because to relate is insecure. And relationship is a security, relationship has a certainty. Relating is just a meeting of two strangers, maybe just an overnight stay, and in the morning we say good-bye. Who knows what is going to happen tomorrow? And we are so afraid that we want to make it certain, we want to make it predictable. We would like tomorrow to be according to our ideas; we don't allow it freedom to have its own say. So we immediately reduce every verb to a noun. You are in love with a woman or a man, and immediately you start thinking of getting married, make it a legal contract. Why?

In a better world, with more meditative people, with a little more enlightenment spread over the earth, people will love, love immensely, but their love will remain a relating, not a relationship. And I am not saying that their love will be only momentary. There is every possibility their love may go deeper than your love, may have a higher quality of intimacy, may have something more of poetry and more of godliness in it. And there is every possibility their love may last longer than your so-called relationship ever lasts. But it will not be guaranteed by the law, by the court, by the policeman. The guarantee will be inner. It will be a commitment from the heart, it will be a silent communion. If you enjoy being with somebody, you will like to enjoy it more and more. If you enjoy the intimacy, you will like to explore the intimacy more and more.

Forget relationships and learn how to relate.

Once you are in a relationship, you start taking each other for granted. That's what destroys all love affairs. Relating means you are always starting; you are continuously trying to become acquainted. Again and again you are introducing yourself to each other. You are trying to see the many facets of the other's personality. You are trying to penetrate deeper and deeper into his realm of inner feelings, into the deep recesses of his being. You are trying to unravel a mystery which cannot be unraveled.

That is the joy of love: the exploration of consciousness. And if you relate, and don't reduce it to a relationship, then the other will become a mirror to you. Exploring him, unawares you will be exploring yourself too. Getting deeper into the other, knowing his feelings, his thoughts, his deeper stirrings, you will be knowing your own deeper stirrings, too. Lovers become mirrors to each other, and then love becomes a meditation.

THE MEDITATIONS:
LOVING YOURSELF,
ONENESS MEDITATION FOR PARTNERS

Here are two related meditations to practice in your own time.

The first, and the most fundamental and relevant for us all, is about loving yourself. Osho often reminds us that love begins with being able to love *ourselves*. Only when we love ourselves are we able to love others; self-love is the foundation.

Technique 1. Loving Yourself

It is best if you can find a beautiful place in nature where you can be alone and undisturbed for a while, but you can also use your favorite spot at home (maybe your favorite chair) or a special meditation place you have created. You can even do it in your bed before going to sleep.

Experiment with this a little:

Just sitting, alone, fall in love with your own self for the first time. Forget the world—just be in love with yourself. Rejoice in your own self, have a taste of yourself . . . Wait a little, search a little. Feel your uniqueness, delight in your own existence. You are in this existence! Even this fact, even this much conscious awareness that "I am" can be a glimpse into bliss—breathing is happening . . . the heart is beating . . . just rejoice in all this a little.

Let the taste of it soak into your every pore. Allow yourself to be swept away by the thrill of it. Start dancing if you feel like dancing, start laughing if you feel like laughing, start singing a song if you feel like singing a song—but remember to remain the center of it all yourself . . . And let the springs of happiness flow from within yourself, not from outside.

Slowly, let this move deep into your experience.

Technique 2. A Oneness Meditation for Partners

The second meditation is meant for couples or friends.

You can do this thirty-minute meditation anytime you feel stuck in your relationship, or just because you would like to make a deeper connection with your friend or partner in a space that is beyond the usual chatter and words. It is recommended to do this at night.

THE FIRST STAGE: Sit facing each other, holding each other's hands crosswise, and for ten minutes, simply look into each other's eyes. If the body starts moving and swaying, allow it. You can blink, but go on looking into each other's eyes. Don't let go of each other's hands whatever happens.

THE SECOND STAGE: Both of you close your eyes and allow the swaying for ten more minutes.

THE THIRD STAGE: Now stand and sway together, holding hands, for ten minutes.

This will mix your energies deeply.

Quote of the Day

Sometimes lovers feel that when love is there, they are not. To feel this in love is easy because love is gratifying, but to feel it in hate is difficult because hate is not gratifying. Lovers, deep lovers, have felt that it is not that they "love"— love is not an activity—rather, they have become love.

—Osho

Notes

DAY 3

Meditations on Anger

Today's program looks at emotions, and specifically at an emotion that we all have experienced—anger.

Our feelings play a profound role in how we view ourselves, and they can even affect our physical health. Often we are trapped in the dilemma between "expression" and "repression." Although expressing an emotion such as anger might frighten or hurt others, by repressing our anger we also risk hurting ourselves. Usually in our lives we deal with anger between these two extremes: either we throw our anger at other people, or we bottle it up, keep it to ourselves, and feel bad.

In today's talk, Osho offers a third alternative, a method that makes it possible to be the master of our emotions rather than being "taken over" by them. After hearing about this approach for dealing with this often unwelcome emotional state, you will be introduced to a simple method that you can use to develop the knack of responding to emotions with awareness rather than just reacting and being overwhelmed by them. Today's practical exercise is specifically geared to changing the "automatic" patterns of anger.

OSHO'S INSIGHT

If you try not to be angry, you will repress anger. If you try to transcend anger, you will not repress anger: on the contrary, you will have to understand anger, you will have to watch anger. In watching is transcendence.

If you repress anger, the anger goes into your unconscious; you become more and more poisoned. It is not good, it is not healthy;

it is going to drive you neurotic sooner or later. And, one day or other, the accumulated anger will explode, and that will be far more dangerous because then it will be absolutely uncontrollable by you.

It is better to be finished with it every day in small doses. Those doses are homeopathic: once in a while you feel angry, be angry. That is far healthier than accumulating anger for a few years then one day exploding. Then it will be too much; you will not be able even to be conscious of what you are doing. It will be absolutely mad. You may do something tremendously harmful to yourself or to somebody else; you may murder or you may commit suicide.

Transcendence is a totally different process. In transcendence you don't repress anger, and you don't express it either.

You know only two ways to deal with anger: expression, repression. And the real way to deal with it is neither. It is not expression, because if you express anger you create anger in the other; then it becomes a chain . . . then the other expresses it, then again you are provoked . . . then where is it going to end? And the more you express, the more it becomes a habit, a mechanical habit. And the more you express it, the more you are practicing it! It will be difficult for you to get out of it.

Out of this fear, repression arose: don't express, because it brings great misery to you, to others—and to no point. It makes you ugly, it creates ugly situations in life, and then you have to pay for all that. And, slowly, slowly, it becomes such a habit that it becomes your second nature.

Out of the fear of expression, repression arose. But if you repress, you are accumulating the poison. It is bound to explode.

The third approach, the approach of all the enlightened people of the world, is neither to express nor repress, but watch. When anger arises, sit silently, let the anger surround you in your inner world, let the cloud surround you, be a silent watcher. See: this is anger.

Buddha has said to his disciples: When anger arises, listen to it, listen to its message. And remember again and again, going on telling yourself: Anger, anger . . . Keep alert, don't fall asleep. Keep alert that anger is surrounding you. You are not it! You are the watcher of it. And that is where the key is.

Slowly, slowly, watching, you become so separate from it that it cannot affect you. And you become so detached from it, and so aloof and so cool and so far away, and the distance is such that it doesn't seem to matter at all. In fact, you will start laughing at all the ridiculous things that you have been doing in the past— because of this anger. It is not you. It is there, outside you. It is surrounding you. But the moment you are dis-identified from it, you will not pour your energy into it.

Remember, we pour our energy into anger; then only does it become vital. It has no energy of its own; it depends on our cooperation. In watching, the cooperation is broken; you are no more supporting it. It will be there, for a few moments, a few minutes, and then it will be gone. Finding no roots in you, finding you unavailable, seeing that you are far away, a watcher on the hills, it will dissipate, it will disappear. And that disappearance is beautiful. That disappearance is a great experience.

Seeing the anger disappear, great serenity arises: the silence that follows the storm. You will be surprised that each time anger arises, and if you can watch, you will fall into such tranquility as you have not known before. You will fall into such deep meditation . . . when the anger disappears you will see yourself so fresh, so young, so innocent, as you have never known yourself. Then you will be thankful even to anger; you will not be angry at it—because it has given you a new beautiful space to live in, a new utterly fresh experience to go through. You have used it, you have made a stepping-stone out of it.

This is the creative use of the negative emotions.

THE MEDITATION:
CHANGING THE PATTERN OF ANGER

It can often seem that anger is just boiling below the surface, waiting for the opportunity to erupt. Even if you throw out your anger and find a way to express it, unless you go more deeply into discovering the source of it—finding what it is inside you that triggers it—the underlying pattern does not change. If all you do is throw it out, afterward you start accumulating anger again, and the pattern continues.

The meditation today is one that can break the pattern that makes us accumulate anger again and again. Given specifically by Osho to an individual who was having trouble with his anger, it is a method that uses your body as your guide. Do it with sincerity, and then see what it brings you. The only way to find that out is to actually do it.

You will need about twenty minutes, and a place where you can be alone without interruption. Set an alarm or timer for fifteen minutes.

The Technique

Each day, for fifteen minutes, at any time you feel is good, close the door to your room and, sitting or standing, start to become angry—but don't release it, don't express it. Go on forcing it, go almost crazy with anger, but don't release it, no expression . . . not even a pillow to hit. Repress it in every way.

At first, you might have to remember a specific situation where you found yourself being really angry, just to bring back the feeling. But let your body be your guide, let the feelings you had in your body be your focus—not whatever circumstance it was that caused the anger in the first place. Don't intellectualize, just stay in touch with the physical sensations that come up when there is anger. And allow those sensations to become more and more intense.

If you feel tension arising in the stomach, as if something is going to explode, pull the stomach in; make it as tense as you can. If you feel the shoulders are becoming tense, your hands want to make a fist, you want to hit somebody, make the shoulders and the hands even more tense and tight. If you find you are clenching your jaw, you want to scream, clench your jaw even tighter. Let the whole body be as tense as possible, almost as if it is a volcano boiling within, but with no release. That is the point to remember—no release, no expression. Don't scream, otherwise the stomach will be released. Don't hit anything, otherwise the shoulders will be released and relaxed. For fifteen minutes get heated up, as if you are trying to reach the boiling point. For fifteen minutes, work the tension up to a climax. When the alarm goes off, try the absolutely hardest you can to keep all the tension inside.

Then, when the alarm has stopped . . . sit silently, close your eyes, relax the body, and just watch what is happening. Be a witness for at least another five minutes, more if it feels right; relax the body, and just watch.

If you find this method suits you, then do this sequence every day for two weeks. This heating of the body system will force your patterns to melt.

And if you feel that anger is not your issue, you can substitute sadness, jealousy, fear—or whatever emotion you would like to change the pattern of—and adjust the exercise accordingly.

Quote of the Day

The science for transformation of life is called
meditation. Through analysis, physical science
reaches the atom and atomic power, but
meditation reaches the soul and soul power.

—Osho

Notes

DAY 3 MEDITATIONS ON ANGER

DAY 4

Living in Balance

The alive person is always moving in polarity: Osho helps us to understand the importance of the interrelationship of polar opposites and how, in terms of the totality of our being, all aspects of our experience—the days and nights, the ups and downs, the joys and sorrows—need to be accepted.

In today's talk, Osho comments on the art of balanced living. Life may be an experience of uncomfortable extremes, but an attachment to the middle, as an ever-static state, may also not be a very good idea. In the meditation that follows Osho's talk, we'll learn how to accept and relax with what we call the "negative" and, paradoxically, how our negative parts add to the taste and spice of life.

OSHO'S INSIGHT

Life consists of extremes. Life is a tension between the opposites. To be exactly in the middle forever means to be dead. The middle is only a theoretical possibility; only once in a while are you in the middle, as a passing phase. It is like walking on a tightrope; you can never be exactly in the middle for any length of time. If you try, you will fall.

To be in the middle is not a static state, it is a dynamic phenomenon.

Balance is not a noun, it is a verb; it is balancing. The tightrope walker continuously moves from the left to the right, from the right to the left. When he feels now he has moved too much to the left and there is fear of falling, he immediately balances himself by moving to the opposite, to the right. Passing from the left to the right, yes, there is a moment when he is in the middle. And again when he has moved too much to the right—there is fear of falling, he is losing balance—he starts moving toward the left. Passing from the right to the left, again he moves through the middle for a moment.

This is what I mean when I say balance is not a noun but a verb—it is balancing, it is a dynamic process. You cannot be in the middle. You can go on moving from left to right and right to left; this is the only way to remain in the middle.

Don't avoid extremes, and don't choose any one extreme. Remain available to both the polarities—that is the art, the secret of balancing. Yes, sometimes be utterly happy, and sometimes be utterly sad: both have their own beauties.

Our mind is a chooser; that's why the problem arises. Remain choiceless. And whatsoever happens and wherever you are, right or left, in the middle or not in the middle, enjoy the moment in its totality. While happy, dance, sing, play music—be happy. And when sadness comes—which is bound to come, which is coming, which has to come, which is inevitable, you cannot avoid it—if you try to avoid it, you will have to destroy the very possibility of happiness. The day cannot be without the night, and the summer cannot be without the winter, and life cannot be without death.

Life contains both: it brings great pain, it also brings great pleasure. Pain and pleasure are two sides of the same coin. If you leave one, you have to leave the other, too. This has been one of the most fundamental misunderstandings down the ages: that you can leave pain and save pleasure, that you can avoid hell and have heaven, that you can avoid the negative and can have only the positive. This is a great fallacy. It is not possible in the very nature of things. The positive and negative are together, inevitably together, indivisibly together. They are two aspects of the same energy.

Can't you see any beauty in sadness? Meditate over it. Next time when you are sad, don't fight with it, don't waste time in fighting. Accept it, welcome it—let it be a welcome guest. And see deep into it, with love, care. Be a real host. And you will be surprised—you will be surprised beyond your comprehension—that sadness has a few beauties which happiness can never have. Sadness has depth, and happiness is always shallow. Sadness has tears, and tears go deeper than any laughter can ever go. And sadness has a silence of its own, a melody, which happiness can never have.

Live life in all possible ways; don't choose one thing against the other, and don't try to be in the middle. And don't try to balance yourself—balance is not something that can be cultivated by you. Balance is something that comes out of the experience of all the dimensions of life.

THE MEDITATION:
ACCEPT THE NEGATIVE AND THE POSITIVE

We have to learn to live with the negative parts of our being as well as the positive; only then do we become whole. Usually, we want to live only with the positive part. But both need to be accepted. This is how life is—both together. In this meditation you practice understanding and accepting all the aspects, good and bad, and allowing a harmony to arise.

When you do this meditation in your own time, take five minutes for each of the three steps. Right now you can have a little taste already, just a few moments for each step.

The Technique

THE FIRST STEP: Close your eyes, and start by looking inside your body, your mind, your feelings: in this moment, where can you find the negative part? It is always there, so just find something "negative," however small it is. And when you find it, don't do anything to get rid of it. Maybe you are feeling restless: so be restless. Or maybe you are feeling cold: so shiver and enjoy it. Or you are feeling hot, so perspire and relax with that. Or you are unhappy about something in your life—be unhappy! Don't make much fuss about it, just be unhappy. Or there is a pain somewhere in the body: let it be there, relax with it. Whatever negative parts you can find, for this moment, relax with them.

THE SECOND STEP: Now let those negative parts go, and, still with eyes closed, start looking inside your body, your mind, your feelings: in this moment, where can you find the positive part? It is there, the other side of the polarity, so find it, however small it is. And when you find it, don't do anything to make it bigger or to hold on to it. Just relax with the positive. Maybe it is the feeling of sitting here comfortably, so enjoy it. Or the fact that you can feel this moment is just for you: relax with it. If a certain memory arises of well-being, or a feeling of lightness—enjoy it . . . and don't make much fuss about it. Accept it in the same way as you did the negative.

THE THIRD STEP: Now let the positive parts go as well and, with eyes still closed, simply be—allowing the harmony between your dark and light parts, allowing the contrasts, the polar opposites of your being. Accepting the dark, accepting the light, understanding that because of the contrasts, life becomes a harmony. For these few moments, just be.

Now you can open your eyes again, and get ready to enjoy the rest of your day with the understanding that balance is something that comes out of the experience of *all* the dimensions of life.

Quote of the Day

Life needs both: thorns and roses, days and
nights, happiness–unhappiness, birth–death.
Be a witness to it all, and you will know
something that is beyond birth, beyond death;
something that is beyond darkness and beyond
light; something that is beyond happiness,
beyond unhappiness. Buddha has called it
peace, nirvana.

—Osho

Notes

DAY 4 LIVING IN BALANCE

DAY 5

*Love and Meditation
Hand in Hand*

In today's excerpt from one of Osho's talks, he offers his insight into what he calls the koan of relationships. As the source of many of the ups and downs, highs and lows, positives and negatives in our lives, our intimate relationships can be quite challenging to navigate. It's often expressed in the familiar line, applied equally to both men and women, "Can't live *with* 'em, can't live *without* 'em." Osho suggests that when we learn to see the partner not as the *cause* of how we feel—happy or miserable, frustrated or content—but rather as a mirror that *shows us who we are*, that understanding brings a whole new quality to the journey of exploring life in partnership with another.

Following the talk, today's meditation technique is called "Allowing the Heart to Open Like a Flower." You can try it whenever time allows.

OSHO'S INSIGHT

A relationship is a koan. And unless you have solved a more fundamental thing about yourself, you cannot solve it. The problem of love can be solved only when the problem of meditation has been solved, not before it, because it is really two non-meditative persons who are creating the problem. Two persons who are in confusion, who don't know who they are, will naturally multiply each other's confusion; they magnify it.

Unless meditation is achieved, love remains a misery. Once you have learned how to live alone, once you have learned how to enjoy your simple existence, for no reason at all, then there is a possibility of solving the second, more complicated problem of two persons being together. Only two meditators can live in love, and then love will not be a koan. But then it will not be a relationship either, in the sense that you understand it. It will be simply a state of love, not a state of relationship.

So, I understand your trouble. But I tell people to go into these troubles because these troubles will make you aware of the fundamental problem—that you, deep inside your being, are a riddle. And the other simply is a mirror. It is difficult to know your own troubles directly; it is very easy to know them in a relationship. A mirror becomes available: you can see your face in the mirror, and the other can see his face in your mirror. Both are angry, because both see ugly faces—and naturally both shout at each other, because their natural logic is, "It is you, this mirror, which is making me look so ugly. Otherwise I am such a beautiful person."

That's the problem that lovers go on trying to solve, and cannot solve. What they are saying again and again is this: "I am such a beautiful person, but you make me look so ugly."

Nobody is making you look ugly—you are ugly! Sorry, but that's how it is. Be thankful to the other; be grateful to the other, because he helps you to see your face.

Don't be angry. Go deeper into yourself, go deeper into meditation.

What happens is that whenever a person is in love he forgets all about meditation. I look at you: whenever I see a few persons missing, I know what has happened to them. Love has happened to them! Now they don't think that they are needed here. They will come only when love creates trouble, and it becomes impossible for them to solve it. Then they will come and ask, "Osho, what to do?"

When you are in love, don't forget meditation. Love is not going to solve anything. Love is only going to show you who you are, where you are. And it is good that love makes you alert—alert of the whole confusion and the chaos within you. Now is the time to meditate. If love and meditation go together, you will have both wings, you will have a balance.

And the vice versa also happens. Whenever a person starts moving deep in meditation, he starts avoiding love, because he thinks if he goes into love his meditation will be disturbed. That too is wrong. Meditation will not be disturbed, meditation will be helped. Why will it be helped? Because love will go on showing you where there are still problems, where they are. Without love, you will become unconscious of your problems. But becoming unconscious does not mean that you have solved them. If there is no mirror, that does not mean that you don't have any face.

Love and meditation should go hand in hand. That is one of the most essential messages that I would like to share with you: Love and meditation should go hand in hand. Love and meditate, meditate and love, and slowly, slowly you will see a new harmony arising in you. Only that harmony will make you contented.

THE MEDITATION:
ALLOWING THE HEART TO OPEN LIKE A FLOWER

This meditation uses the breathing . . . which is happening all the time, even though for the most part we are not aware of it.

Take a moment now and loosen your clothing, especially around the stomach so that this area can move more freely.

"Sometimes the heart full of love is there," says Osho, ". . . but it is like a bud, not like a flower, the petals are closed. This bud can become a flower."

It should be noted here that there is a heart muscle, and there is a heart center—sometimes called a heart chakra or heart center—located between the breasts. In this meditation we are dealing with the heart center. And if you like, you can imagine your heart center as a flower of your choice.

This is a small and simple breathing technique to help the heart center to flower.

The Technique

Sit in a relaxed position while keeping your spine straight.

Take a moment and become aware of your breathing . . . not to change it, but to become more aware it, of HOW it is happening.

Is it deep, or is it shallow? . . . Is it happening on its own? Or do you observe that you make an effort to breathe in . . . or to breathe out? Do you feel more comfortable on the inhalation or on the exhalation?

Now we are going to breathe in a particular way. How it works will be explained first, and then you can close your eyes and practice.

First of all, exhale till ALL the air is out of the lungs; then pull in your stomach, and use that action to push out any remaining air.

When you feel all the air is out, pause and let your lungs remain empty for as long as possible. (No need to be afraid, because whenever necessary, the air will come rushing back in by itself.)

When the air comes rushing back in, it will open the petals of the heart center. This is one of the most significant devices to open the heart.

So get ready now:

Exhale deeply, pull in your stomach, and throw ALL the air out of your lungs.

When you feel all the air is out, keep it out as long as you can . . . let it remain out as long as possible.

. . . And when the air comes rushing back in, feel it opening the petals of the heart.

Now do it once more:

Exhale deeply, pull in your stomach, and throw ALL the air out of your lungs.

When you feel all the air is out, keep it out as long as you can . . . let it remain out as long as possible.

And when the air comes rushing back in, feel it opening the petals of the heart.

This simple technique can also be used whenever you want to change your mood—maybe you're feeling jealous, or annoyed with something at work, or upset by something someone has said to you. Just take a few moments and throw all the air out of your lungs . . . and with it, all the negativity you are feeling. Throw it out. And when the air comes rushing back in, allow the petals of your heart to open.

Quote of the Day

Meditation is the beginning, the seed; ecstasy
is the flower. And by meditation I mean not
looking through the mind—it is the mind that
cuts you away from the world, but looking
through the heart. It is the heart that joins
you with the world, it is the heart that has the
courage to melt and merge with the whole. The
mind is a coward, the heart is really courageous.

—Osho

Notes

DAY 5 LOVE AND MEDITATION HAND IN HAND

DAY 6

Living Dangerously

Nearly all of us have a "comfort zone" where we feel safe, secure, and as if we have everything pretty much under control. But sometimes, that comfort zone can become a prison, a place where nothing ever seems to change, where day after day we find ourselves going round and round in the same routines. When that happens, it's no wonder that we feel "stuck." Today's program invites us to step outside the comfort zone of the familiar, the safe and secure. In his talk, Osho responds to the question, "What does it mean to live dangerously?" His answer may surprise you.

The meditation that follows is an exercise in dropping the "armor" that can build up around us when we are afraid to step outside our comfort zone. An experiment in shedding this layer of protection, which can be practiced in the safe environment of our own home, can make it possible to meet people and encounter the unfamiliar in a new, more intimate, less formal way.

OSHO'S INSIGHT

What does it mean to live dangerously?

To live dangerously means to live. If you don't live dangerously, you don't live. Living flowers only in danger. Living never flowers in security; it flowers only in insecurity.

If you start getting secure, you become a stagnant pool. Then your energy is no more moving. Then you are afraid, because one never knows how to go into the unknown. And why take the risk? The known is more secure. Then you get obsessed with the familiar. You go on getting fed up with it, you are bored with it, you feel miserable in it, but still it seems familiar and comfortable. At least it is known. The unknown creates a trembling in you—the very idea of the unknown, and you start feeling unsafe.

There are only two types of people in the world. People who want to live comfortably—they are seeking death; they want a comfortable grave. And people who want to live—they choose to live dangerously, because life thrives only when there is risk.

Have you ever gone climbing in the mountains? The higher the climb, the fresher you feel, the younger you feel. The greater the danger of falling, the bigger the abyss by the side, the more alive you are . . . between life and death, when you are just hanging between life and death. Then there is no boredom, then there is no dust of the past, no desire for the future. Then the present moment is very sharp, like a flame. It is enough. You live in the here and now.

Or surfing . . . or skiing . . . or gliding. Wherever there is a risk of losing life, there is tremendous joy, because the risk of losing life makes you tremendously alive. Hence people are attracted to dangerous sports.

Reaching higher, going farther away from the settled, the routine life, you again become wild, you again become part of the animal world. And each moment the security, the bank balance, the wife, the husband, the family, the society, the church, the respectability . . . all are fading away and away, distant and distant. You become alone.

This is why people are so much interested in sports. But that too is not real danger, because you can become very, very skilled. And then these risks are only physical risks, only the body is involved. When I say to you, live dangerously, I mean not only bodily risk, but psychological risk, and finally spiritual risk.

When I say live dangerously, I mean don't live the life of ordinary respectability—that you are a mayor in a town, or a member of the corporation. This is not life. When everything is going perfectly well, simply see it—you are dying and nothing is happening. Watch: one can miss one's whole life for ordinary, mundane things.

To be spiritual means to understand that these small things should not be given too much importance. I am not saying that they are meaningless. Money is needed, it is a need, but money is not the goal and cannot be the goal. A house is needed, certainly. It is a need. I am not an ascetic, and I don't want you to destroy your houses and escape to the Himalayas.

People come to me and they say they feel very bored. They feel fed up, stuck. What to do? They think that just by repeating a mantra they will become again alive. It is not so easy. They will have to change their whole life pattern.

Love, but don't let your love degrade into marriage. Work—work is needed—but don't let work become your only life. Play should remain your life, your center of life. Work should be as a means toward play. Work in the office, and work in the factory, and work in the shop, but just to have time, opportunity, to play. Don't let your life be reduced into just a working routine. Because the goal of life is play. Play means doing something for its own sake.

To live dangerously means to live life as if each moment is its own end. Each moment has its own intrinsic value. And you are not afraid. You know death is there, and you accept the fact that death is there, and you are not hiding against death. In fact, you go and encounter death. You enjoy those moments of encountering death—physically, psychologically, spiritually.

Enjoying those moments where you come directly in contact with death, where death becomes almost a reality, is what I mean when I say live dangerously.

Love brings you face to face with death. Meditation brings you face to face with death.

But remember one thing—never forget the art of risking, never, never. Always remain capable of risking. Wherever you can find an opportunity to risk, never miss it, and you will never be a loser. Risk is the only guarantee for being truly alive.

THE MEDITATION:
DISSOLVING THE ARMOR

Today's meditation is about dissolving a layer of protection, a certain type of invisible armor with which we have learned to face the world: our "risk-free" zone.

One of the ways we protect ourselves from situations or people that feel threatening is to create a kind of armor around ourselves, a "protective shield" that helps us feel less vulnerable, safer and more secure. It's easy to see this in others—we even have a common expression to describe it; when a person who is normally shy and timid starts to speak up, we say, "she's coming out of her shell."

Sometimes, this armor can be useful, even necessary. But the problem is that it often becomes a habit, a pattern, almost like a second skin that keeps us from feeling fully alive, spontaneous, playful, confident in ourselves and who we are. But it has been with us so long, we don't know how to get out of it—although we should, in fact, be able to take it off as easily as we put it on.

A woman came to Osho with just this difficulty, and this is what he said:

"You carry an armor around you. It is just an armor. It is not clinging to you—*you* are clinging to *it*. So when you become aware of it, you can simply drop it. The armor is dead: if you don't carry it, it will disappear."

He goes on to suggest ways to start becoming more aware of this armor, using a meditation technique that brings awareness to where the armor is expressed in the body.

The Technique

There are three parts to the meditation, as follows:

THE FIRST STAGE: Walking or sitting, exhale deeply. The emphasis should be on exhalation, not on inhalation. So exhale deeply—as much air as you can throw out, throw. Exhale through the mouth but do it slowly so it takes time. The longer it takes the better, because then it goes deeper. When all the air inside the body is thrown out, then the body inhales; don't *you* inhale. The exhalation should be slow and deep, and the inhalation should be fast.

This will change the armor near the chest.

THE SECOND STAGE: Start a little running, jogging, or walking at a brisk pace. And while your legs are in movement, just visualize that a load is disappearing from the legs, as if it is falling off them. When our freedom has been restricted too much, our legs carry the armor. So start running, jogging, walking, or even unstructured dancing, and as the legs are moving, feel that armor around them falling off. And again, as in the first step, put more attention on the exhalation of your breath.

Once you regain your legs and their fluidity, you will have a tremendous energy flow.

THE THIRD STAGE: When you are ready to go to sleep at night, take off your clothes, and while taking them off, simply imagine that you are not only taking off your clothes, you are taking off your armor, too. Actually do it. Take the clothes off, and have another good deep exhalation while letting that armor dissolve.

Quote of the Day

When the seed becomes a sprout it is going into
something unknown. When the sprout starts
growing flowers it is again a movement into
the unknown. And when the fragrance leaves
the flowers—again, a quantum leap into the
unknown. Life needs courage at each step.

—Osho

Notes

DAY 6 LIVING DANGEROUSLY

DAY 7

Watching the Mind

The essence of all methods of meditation is to watch, observe, witness, and be mindful. What stops us from being able to access that natural state of being (which is why we need to have "methods"!) is our complete and automatic immersion in the process of our thoughts and feelings—collectively called the mind.

We seem to have lost the "off switch" for the mind, and so our thoughts and preoccupations are relentless companions that we can't seem to get away from. Even when the body is tired, often thoughts will keep us sleepless. Interestingly, Osho includes the emotions, along with the thoughts, in what is called "the mind." We have all probably experienced how this "thinking and feeling machine" can drive us crazy. We've also all likely thought that it would be just great if we knew how to turn it off at will and have some peace and quiet when thinking isn't actually needed.

Osho has spoken a lot about the mind, and the people around him have asked him many questions related to it. In today's excerpt, Osho responds to a question about whether the mind cannot simply "commit suicide." The questioner is clearly hoping that there is some shortcut to be found for silencing the mind. Osho responds with a beautiful explanation about the relationship of mind and meditation.

In the practical Osho meditations that follow, one suggests we embrace our thought processes and start enjoying the mind, rather than fighting with it; the other gives an effective, immediate, STOP method that creates a distance between us and our thinking.

OSHO'S INSIGHT

Can the mind commit suicide?

The mind cannot commit suicide, because whatsoever the mind can do will strengthen the mind. Any doing on the part of the mind makes the mind more strong. So suicide is impossible.

Mind doing something means mind continuing itself—so that is not in the nature of things. But suicide happens. Mind cannot commit it, mm? Let me make it absolutely clear: mind cannot commit it, but suicide happens. It happens through watching the mind, not by doing anything.

The watcher is separate from the mind. It is deeper than the mind, higher than the mind. The watcher is always hidden behind the mind. A thought passes, a feeling arises—who is watching this thought? Not the mind itself, because mind is nothing but the process of thought and feeling. The mind is just the traffic of thinking. Who is watching it? When you say, "An angry thought has arisen in me," who are "you"? In whom has the thought arisen? Who is the container? The thought is the content—who is the container?

The mind is like when you print a book: on white, clean paper, words appear. That empty paper is the container and the printed words are the content. Consciousness is like empty paper. Mind is like written, printed paper.

Whatsoever exists as an object inside you, whatsoever you can see and observe, is the mind. The observer is not the mind, the observed is the mind. So if you can go on simply observing, without condemning, without in any way creating a conflict with the mind, without indulging it, without following it, without going against it—if you can simply be there, indifferent to it, in that indifference suicide happens. It is not that mind commits suicide: when the watcher arises, the witness is there—mind simply disappears.

Mind exists with your cooperation or your conflict. Both are ways of cooperating—conflict too! When you fight with the mind, you are giving energy to it. In your very fight you have accepted the mind; in your very fighting you have accepted the power of the mind over your being. So whether you cooperate or you conflict, in both the cases the mind becomes stronger and stronger.

Just watch. Just be a witness. And, by and by, you will see gaps arising. A thought passes, and another thought does not come immediately—there is an interval. In that interval is peace. In that interval is love. In that interval is all that you have always been seeking and never finding. In that gap you are no more an ego. In that gap you are not defined, confined, imprisoned. In that gap you are vast, immense, huge. In that gap you are one with existence—the barrier exists not. Your boundaries are no more there. You melt into existence, and the existence melts in you. You start overlapping.

If you go on watching and you don't get attached to these gaps either . . . because that is natural now, to get attached to these gaps. If you start hankering for these gaps . . . because they are tremendously beautiful, they are immensely blissful. It is natural to get attached to them, and desire arises to have more and more of these gaps—then you will miss, then your watcher has disappeared. Then those gaps will again disappear, and again the traffic of the mind will be there.

So the first thing is to become an indifferent watcher. And the second thing is to remember that when beautiful gaps arise, don't get attached to them; don't start asking for them, don't start waiting that they should happen more often. If you can remember these two things—when beautiful gaps come, watch them too, and keep your indifference alive—then one day the traffic simply disappears with the road, they both disappear. And there is tremendous emptiness.

That's what Buddha calls *nirvana*—the mind has ceased. This is what I call suicide—but the mind has not committed it. Mind cannot commit it. You can help it to happen. You can hinder it, you can help it to happen—it depends on you, not on your mind. All that mind can do will always strengthen the mind.

So meditation is not really mind-effort. Real meditation is not effort at all. Real meditation is just allowing the mind to have its own way and not interfering in any way whatsoever—just remaining watchful, witnessing. It silences, by and by, it becomes still. One day it is gone. You are left alone.

That aloneness is what your reality is. And in that aloneness nothing is excluded, remember it. In that aloneness everything is included.

THE MEDITATIONS:
ENJOY THE MIND, AND . . . STOP!

The first meditation technique is taken from a suggestion by Osho to a man who came with the following complaint: "I'm so fed up with my mind. I feel I'm never here, and I never see anything at all. I try everything: I try meditation, I try to be aware, but often I don't feel it." Osho responds by pointing out that the questioner is, in a way, trying to go against his nature—he's a "mind person," not a "heart person," and if he tries to change himself he will just make himself miserable. Then, he offers an alternative.

Technique 1. Enjoy the Mind

Don't try to stop your thinking. It is a very natural part of you; you will go crazy if you try to stop it. It would be like a tree trying to stop its leaves; the tree would go mad.

But just letting your thoughts flow is still not enough; the second step is to enjoy thinking, to play with it! By playing with it, enjoying it, and welcoming it, you will start becoming more alert about it, more aware of it, without any effort, very indirectly. When you are trying to become aware, the mind distracts you and you become angry with it—and again the conflict and friction start that strengthen the mind.

So this method is to start enjoying the thought process. Just see the nuances of thoughts, the turns they take, how one thing leads to another, how they get hooked into each other. It is really a miracle to watch! Just a small thought can take you on a long journey. A dog starts barking and your thought process is triggered. The dog is forgotten; you remember a friend who had a beautiful dog. Now you are off! Then the friend is forgotten; you remember the friend's wife who was beautiful, and so you go on, and then other women. . . . Where you will end, nobody knows; and it all started with a dog barking!

Enjoy it. Let it be a game; play it deliberately and you will be surprised—sometimes just enjoying it, you will find beautiful pauses. Suddenly you will find that, for instance, a dog is barking and nothing is arising in your mind, no chain of thinking starts. The dog goes on barking and you go on listening and no thought arises. Small gaps will arise . . . they come on their own, and when they come, they are beautiful. In those small gaps you will start watching the watcher—and it will be natural. Again thoughts will start, and you will enjoy that. Go on easily, take it easy.

Now the second technique:

Technique 2. STOP!

And now, for a moment: if you are not already standing, stand up . . . and: STOP!

Stop completely, no movement—and just be present to whatever is happening. Be aware of whatever sounds and sights are surrounding you, whatever feelings might be arising in you. Just a few seconds are enough, no need to force yourself to stay still—only long enough to bring yourself into the present moment.

Very good—that gave you a taste of Osho's STOP exercise— and your homework for today's segment: we suggest you do this STOP! exercise at least five more times before you resume the course tomorrow. Don't plan it, or set a time for it, just whenever you remember—washing dishes, walking down the street, putting on your shoes, any small daily activity—STOP!

Plus: whenever you remember—enjoy watching the mind.

Quote of the Day

This is the only distinction between the dream
and the real: reality allows you to doubt,
and the dream does not allow you to doubt. . . .
To me, the capacity to doubt is one of the
greatest blessings to humanity.

—Osho

Notes

DAY 7 WATCHING THE MIND

DAY 8

It Needs Intelligence to Be Happy

We often first get interested in meditation because we're seeking some peace, or that elusive state of well-being called happiness—qualities that always seem to take a back seat to stress, worry, hurry, or just "the daily grind." Deep down everyone wants to be happy, and luckily our inner intelligence will keep on looking for it, as it can sense it is part of our birthright.

In response to a question about why it is so difficult to be happy, Osho talks about "happiness" and "misery," and turns the conventional wisdom about these seeming polar opposites on its head. As is often the case, he comes to the question from a quite unexpected point of view.

The meditation that follows his insight is a simple technique that will support your innate, natural quality of happiness as you go about your day.

OSHO'S INSIGHT

Why is it so difficult to be happy?

Misery has many things to give to you which happiness cannot give. On the contrary, happiness takes away many things from you. In fact, happiness takes all that you have ever had, all that you have ever been; happiness destroys you. Misery nourishes your ego, and happiness is basically a state of egolessness. That is the problem, the very crux of the problem. That's why people find it very difficult to be happy.

If this is understood then things become very clear. Misery makes you special. Happiness is a universal phenomenon, there is nothing special about it. Trees are happy, and animals are happy, and birds are happy. The whole existence is happy except man. Being miserable, man becomes very special, extraordinary.

When you are ill, depressed, in misery, friends come to visit you, to solace you, to console you. When you are happy, the same friends become jealous of you. When you are really happy, you will find the whole world has turned against you. Nobody likes a happy person, because the happy person hurts the egos of the others. The others start feeling, "So you have become happy and we are still crawling in darkness, misery, and hell. How dare you be happy when we are all in such misery!"

Look into your misery and you will find certain fundamental things are there. One: it gives you respect. People feel more friendly towards you, more sympathetic. You will have more friends if you are miserable. This is a very strange world, something is fundamentally wrong with it. It should not be so; the happy person should have more friends. But become happy, and people become jealous of you; they are no longer friendly. They feel cheated; you have something that is not available to them— why are you happy? So we have learned down the ages a subtle mechanism: to repress happiness and to express misery.

You have to learn how to be happy, and you have to learn to respect happy people, and you have to learn to pay more attention to happy people, remember. This is a great service to humanity. Don't sympathize too much with people who are miserable. If somebody is miserable, help, but don't sympathize. Don't give him the idea that misery is something worthwhile.

We have to learn a totally new language, only then this old rotten humanity can be changed. We have to learn the language of health, wholeness, happiness. It is going to be difficult because our investments are great.

That is why it is so difficult to be happy and so easy to be miserable. One thing more: misery needs no talents, anybody can afford it. Happiness needs talents, genius, creativity. Only creative people are happy.

Let this sink deep in your heart: only creative people are happy. Happiness is a by-product of creativity. Create something, and you will be happy. Write a poem, sing a song, dance a dance, and see: you start becoming happy.

It needs intelligence to be happy. The intelligent person is rebellious. Intelligence is rebellion; without intelligence there can be no happiness. Man can only be happy if he is intelligent, utterly intelligent.

Meditation is a device to release your intelligence. The more meditative you become, the more intelligent you become. But remember, by intelligence I don't mean intellectuality. Intellectuality is part of stupidity. Intelligence is a totally different phenomenon, it has nothing to do with the head. Intelligence is something that comes from your very center. It wells up in you, and with it, many things start growing in you. You become happy, you become creative, you become rebellious, you become adventurous, you start loving insecurity. You start moving into the unknown. You start living dangerously, because that is the only way to live. . . . To decide that "I will live my life intelligently," that "I will not be just an imitator," that "I will live within my own being, I will not be directed and commanded from without," that "I will risk all to be myself, but I will not be part of a mob psychology," that "I will walk alone," that "I will find my own path," that "I will make my own path in the world of truth." Just by walking into the unknown you create the path. The path is not already there; just by walking, you create it.

Intelligence gives you the courage to be alone, and intelligence gives you the vision to be creative. A great urge, a great hunger arises to be creative. And only then, as a consequence, you can be happy, you can be blissful.

THE MEDITATION:
INNER SMILE

Today's meditation is a practice that supports our capacity to enter into a state of simple, ordinary egolessness—a part of "the language of health, wholeness, happiness" Osho mentions above.

You can do this meditation for just a few minutes, whenever you have the time and are sitting somewhere without any specific task at hand. You can do it on the subway, at home, during your lunch break at work, while watching your toddler play in the park, anytime when you are basically idle. In the beginning, while learning, it's good to do it with eyes closed. Later on you can easily do it with eyes open also—and then no one around you will even notice that you are doing a meditation technique while sitting there.

The Technique

THE FIRST STAGE: Whenever you have nothing specific to do, sit and relax the lower jaw. Let your mouth open just slightly. Start breathing from the mouth, but not deeply. Simply let the body breathe so the breathing becomes more and more shallow. And when you feel that the breath has become very shallow, and your mouth is open and your jaw relaxed, your whole body will feel very relaxed.

THE SECOND STAGE: Now start feeling a smile—not on your face but all over your being—and you will be able to. It is not a smile that comes on the lips; it is an existential smile that spreads just inside.

Try it out and then you will know what it is—because it cannot be explained. No need to smile with your lips, on your face, but just as if you are smiling from the belly; the belly is smiling. And it is a smile, not laughter, so it is very very soft, delicate, fragile—like a small rosebud opening in the belly and the fragrance spreads all over the body.

THE THIRD STAGE: Once you have known what this smile is, you can remain happy for twenty-four hours. And whenever you feel that you are missing that happiness, just close your eyes for a few moments and catch hold of that smile again, and it will be there. In the daytime, as many times as you want, you can catch hold of it. It is always there.

Quote of the Day

Meditation is fire—it burns your thoughts, your desires, your memories; it burns the past and the future. It burns your mind and the ego. It takes away all that you think that you are. It is a death and a rebirth, a crucifixion and a resurrection. You are born anew. You lose your old identity totally, and you attain to a new vision of life.

—Osho

Notes

DAY 8 IT NEEDS INTELLIGENCE TO BE HAPPY

DAY 9

Integration of Body, Mind, and Soul

In addition to his many books, all transcribed from his talks, Osho is known for his revolutionary "active meditations." Just sitting silently can be very difficult for people who live in an environment that places complex demands on their time, dealing with many different situations and people throughout the day, as most of us do. To be able to spend "quality time" with ourselves, first we need to get rid of the accumulated tensions of body and mind; otherwise, built-up thoughts, worries, and tensions will just clamor for our attention as soon as we try to sit.

Happily, Osho points out, running, swimming, and dancing can each be doorways to meditation. If we go into these activities with awareness and do them totally, they naturally bring a unity of body, mind, and consciousness. And that's what meditation is really all about.

After an introduction from Osho about the importance of bringing the energies of body, mind, and spirit together, today's meditation technique can give you a firsthand taste of what that feels like.

OSHO'S INSIGHT

Modern physics has discovered one of the greatest things ever discovered, and that is that matter is energy. That is the greatest contribution of Albert Einstein to humanity:

Existence is energy. Science has discovered that the observed is energy, the object is energy. Down the ages, at least for five thousand years, it has been known that the other polarity—the subject, the observer, consciousness—is energy. Your body is energy, your mind is energy, your soul is energy.

If all these three energies function in harmony, you are healthy and whole. If these energies don't function in harmony and accord, you are ill, unhealthy, you are no longer whole. The effort that we are making here is how to help you so that your body, your mind, your consciousness, can all dance in one rhythm, in a togetherness, in a deep harmony—not in conflict at all, but in cooperation.

People are living in chaos: their bodies say one thing, their bodies want to go in one direction; their minds are completely oblivious of the body—because for centuries you have been taught that you are not the body, for centuries you have been told that the body is your enemy, that you have to fight with it, that you have to destroy it, that the body is sin—you don't experience your body in a rhythmic dance with yourself.

Hence my insistence on dancing and music, because it is only in dance that you will feel that your body, your mind, and you are functioning together. And the joy is infinite when all these function together; the richness is great.

You have to learn how to play on these three energies so that they all become an orchestra.

It happens many times that runners . . . You will not think of running as a meditation, but runners sometimes have felt a tremendous experience of meditation. And they were surprised, because they were not looking for it but it has happened, and now running is becoming more and more a new kind of meditation. It can happen in running. If you have ever been a runner, if you have enjoyed running in the early morning when the air is fresh and young, and the whole world is coming back out of sleep, awakening, and you were running and your body was functioning beautifully, and the fresh air, and the new world again born out of the darkness of the night, and everything singing all around, and you were feeling so alive . . . A moment comes when the runner disappears, there is only running. The body, mind, and soul start functioning together; suddenly an inner orgasm is released.

My own observation is that a runner can more easily come close to meditation than anybody else. Jogging can be of immense help, swimming can be of immense help. All these things have to be transformed into meditations.

Drop old ideas of meditations, that just sitting underneath a tree with a yoga posture is meditation. That is only one of the ways, and may be suitable for a few people but is not suitable for all. For a small child it is not meditation, it is torture. For a young man who is alive, vibrant, it is repression, it is not meditation. Maybe for an old man who has lived, whose energies are declining, it may be meditation.

People differ, there are many types of people.

Running can be a meditation—jogging, dancing, swimming, anything can be a meditation. My definition of meditation is: whenever your body, mind, soul are functioning together in rhythm it is meditation. And if you are alert that you are doing it as a meditation—not to take part in the Olympics, but doing it as a meditation—then it is tremendously beautiful.

My effort is to make meditation available to each and everybody; whosoever wants to meditate, meditation should be made available according to his type. If he needs rest, then rest should be his meditation. Then "sitting silently doing nothing, and the spring comes and the grass grows by itself"—that will be his meditation. We have to find as many dimensions to meditation as there are people in the world. And the pattern has not to be very rigid, because no two individuals are alike. The pattern has to be very liquid so that it can fit with the individual. In the past, the practice was that the individual had to fit with the pattern.

I bring a revolution. The individual has not to fit with the pattern, the pattern has to fit with the individual. My respect for the individual is absolute.

But the basic fundamental is, whatsoever the meditation, it has to fill this requirement: that the body, mind, consciousness, all three should function in unity.

THE MEDITATION:
IMAGINE RUNNING

If running, swimming, or maybe bicycling is already part of your life, something you do regularly to "clear your head" and recharge your batteries, perhaps what Osho has just talked about sparked a recognition in you. You already have a key in your hand—now your job is to use it with more intention and greater awareness.

Even if your form of physical exercise is to go to a gym and work out on the treadmill . . . take a look at how you approach it, and consider making it a meditation. Turn off the television screen on the treadmill, leave the book in your bag in the locker room. If you listen to music, put a soundtrack together that is purely energetic and supportive of your physical activity, instead of triggering your mind and emotions. If your gym imposes a soundtrack on everyone, take some earplugs with you. Anything you can do to support giving your full attention and energy to the physical activity will help lead you to the space Osho is talking about.

Now, the specific technique for today, which may surprise you:

The Technique

If for some reason you cannot run, you don't have the space or the time, maybe you aren't feeling well, the weather is lousy, or you've injured yourself, try this:

Lie on your bed and imagine that you are running. Just imagine the whole scene—the trees and the wind caressing your face, the sun, the beach, the salty air. . . . everything, visualize it and make it as colorful as possible.

Perhaps you have a memory of a beautiful morning in the past—running on the beach, in the woods—imagine running, running, running . . . Soon you will find that your breathing is changing . . . and you keep going on and on . . . you can go on like this for miles on end . . .

And you will be surprised that even doing this on the bed, you might attain to moments when suddenly meditation, silence, inner peace is there.

Then . . . after maybe fifteen, twenty minutes . . .

Let the running come to an end and be still. Take a deep breath and rest for a while—watch within and without.

Quote of the Day

Learn the art of celebrating yourself—for no
reason, for no cause. Just to be is enough, more
than enough. To be part of the whole is such a
great metamorphosis that you cannot resist—
you have to dance, you have to sing, you have to
express your joy, your blissfulness.

—Osho

Notes

DAY 9 INTEGRATION OF BODY, MIND, AND SOUL

DAY 10

Slowing Down

Technology is meant to make life easier, but the reality for many of us is that life today is busier than ever before: we are on call round the clock, checking texts, emails, blogs, social media posts, and news, from morning till night.

Compared to people who lived at the time of Buddha, or even just a hundred years ago, life is a constant whirl of activity and sensory stimulation. We are on the run all the time.

Today's program of meditation is about relearning the art of slowing down.

In explaining how meditation can be a great help in slowing down, Osho examines what we have been taught about the importance of setting goals, keeping busy, and our fears of being called "lazy" or lacking in ambition. Ultimately, if we can begin to see these internalized attitudes for what they are, we can begin to understand that each moment lived with our total presence in the moment is exactly where we're meant to be.

Today's meditation, titled "Surround Yourself with a Climate of Joy," is an experiment in creating our own space, a center of joy that remains relaxed even in the midst of the cyclone of the outer world.

OSHO'S INSIGHT

How to slow down?

Life is not going anywhere; there is no goal to it, no destination. Life is non-purposive, it simply is. Unless this understanding penetrates your heart, you cannot slow down.

Slowing down is not a question of any "how"; it is not a question of technique, method.

We reduce everything into a how. There is a great how-to-ism all over the world, and every person, particularly the modern contemporary mind, has become a how-to-er: how to do this, how to do that, how to grow rich, how to be successful, how to influence people and win friends, how to meditate, even how to love. The day is not far off when some stupid guy is going to ask how to breathe.

It is not a question of *how* at all. Don't reduce life into technology. Life reduced into technology loses all flavor of joy.

I have come across a book; the name of the book is hilarious. Its name is *You Must Relax*. Try to relax, and you will find that you feel more tense than ever. Try harder, and you will feel more and more tense.

Relaxation is not a consequence, is not a result of some activity; it is the glow of understanding.

Live in the moment for the sheer joy of living it. Then each moment has the quality of an orgasm. Yes, it is orgasmic. You are here to enjoy life to its fullness. And the only way to live, love, enjoy, is to forget the future. It exists not.

Life is a pilgrimage to nowhere: from nowhere to nowhere. And between these two nowheres is the now-here. Nowhere consists of two words: now, here. Between these two nowheres is the now-here.

It is not a question of following a certain technique to slow down, because if your basic approach towards life remains the same—goal-oriented—you may try to slow down, and you may even succeed in slowing down, but now you have started another tension in your life. You have to be constantly on guard so that you remain slow; you have to hold yourself continuously so that you remain slow.

How can you slow down? If you slow down you will be a failure; if you slow down you will never be able to succeed. If you slow down you are lost! If you slow down you will be anonymous, you will not be able to leave your signature in the world. Who will you be if you slow down? Everybody else is not slowing down.

It is almost as if you are in an Olympic race and you ask me, "How to slow down?" If you slow down, you are a drop-out! Then you are no longer in the Olympic race. And this whole life has been turned into an Olympic race. Everybody is racing, and everybody has to race to the optimum, because it is a question of life and death. Millions of enemies . . . we are living in a world where everybody is your enemy, because with whomsoever you are in competition, they are your enemies.

Meditation is not something that can grow in any soil. It needs a basic understanding; the change has to be very fundamental. It needs a new soil to grow in; it needs a new gestalt.

A meditator naturally slows down with no effort. He does not practice it. A practiced thing is never true; it is artificial, arbitrary. Avoid practiced things—at the most they can be acting, they are not true. And only truth liberates.

This is the only moment there is, and this is the only reality there is, and this is the only reality that has always been and will always be.

Change your basic philosophy, which is now that of an achiever. Relax into your being. Don't have any ideals, don't try to make something out of yourself. You are perfect as you are. With all your imperfections, you are perfect. If you are imperfect, you are perfectly imperfect—but perfection is there.

THE MEDITATION:

SURROUND YOURSELF WITH A CLIMATE OF JOY

If this method suits you, then practice it for a few minutes each night over a period of three weeks, also carrying it loosely with you during the day. Later on you can drop the nightly practice, and by and by, the method will dissolve as its lessons become integrated into your life.

The Technique

FIRST WEEK: Lying down or sitting on your bed, switch the light off and be in darkness. Remember any beautiful moment that you have experienced in the past—just choose your favorite. It may be very ordinary, because sometimes extraordinary things happen in very ordinary situations: sitting still, doing nothing, the rain falling on the roof . . . the smell, the sound . . . you are surrounded—and something clicks: you are in a sacred moment. Or one day walking along the road, suddenly the sunlight falls on you from behind the trees . . . and click: something opens; for a moment you are transported into another world.

Close your eyes and relive that moment. Go into the details—the sounds . . . the smells . . . the very texture of the moment . . . A bird is singing, a dog is barking . . . the wind is blowing, the sounds. Go into all the experiences, from all the sides; multidimensional, from all the senses. Once you have chosen your beautiful moment, continue the meditation for seven nights.

You will find that every night you are moving into deeper details—things that you may even have missed in the real moment, but that your mind has recorded. You may feel subtle nuances that you were not aware you had experienced. You may come to recognize that they were there, but you had missed them in that moment. The mind records it all; it is a very reliable servant, tremendously capable.

By the seventh day you will be able to see your beautiful moment so clearly, you will feel you have never seen any moment as clearly as this.

SECOND WEEK: Continue as before, and add one more thing: Feel the space of that moment around you . . . feel the climate is surrounding you from all sides—up to three feet around you. Feel an aura of that moment surrounding you. By the fourteenth day you may be able to be in a totally different world; and still conscious that beyond those three feet, a different time and a different dimension are present.

THIRD WEEK: Add one more thing: Live the moment, be surrounded by it, and now create an imaginary antispace. For example, you are feeling very good; for three feet you are surrounded by that goodness, that joyful space. Now think of a situation, as in the following.

Somebody insults you—but the insult comes only up to the limit of the space. There is a fence, and the insult cannot enter you. It comes like an arrow . . . and falls there. Or remember some sad moment: You are hurt, but that hurt comes up to the glass wall that is surrounding you and falls there. It never reaches you.

If the first two weeks have gone right, by the third week you will be able to see that everything stops at that three-foot limit and nothing penetrates you.

FOURTH WEEK AND BEYOND: Now continue to keep that aura with you; going to the marketplace, talking to people, continuously have it in mind. And you will be thrilled; you will move in the world having your own world, a private world continuously with you that will make you capable of living in the present— calm, quiet, centered.

Carry that aura for a few days, a few months. When you see that it is no longer needed, you can drop it. Once you know how to be here now, once you have enjoyed the beauty of it, the tremendous bliss of it, you can drop the aura of it.

Quote of the Day

Women can wait, and they can wait infinitely,
their patience is infinite. It has to be so, because
a child has to be carried for nine months. And
look at a mother, a woman who is just about
to be a mother: she becomes more beautiful,
she attains a different type of grace, an aura
surrounds her. Now she is blooming, soon she
will flower.

—Osho

Notes

DAY 11

Everybody Is Creative

Today's program challenges our self-limiting ideas about creativity. We live in a culture that assumes a person must have a special talent, a unique gift, a mastery of some technique in order to be creative. Osho challenges this notion, insisting that creativity is first and foremost an approach to life, a knack of bringing joy to whatever we are doing in the moment, whether that is cooking a meal, cleaning the floor, washing the dishes, or having a quiet chat with a friend.

The meditation for today is called "From Gibberish to Silence." Fun, playful, energizing—you can think of it as a technique to create a blank canvas for the art of your life, a way to empty out all the ideas you've been given about what it means to be creative.

OSHO'S INSIGHT

Creativity has nothing to do with any activity in particular—with painting, poetry, dancing, singing. It has nothing to do with anything in particular.

Anything can be creative—you bring that quality to the activity. Activity itself is neither creative nor uncreative. You can paint in an uncreative way; you can sing in an uncreative way. You can clean the floor in a creative way; you can cook in a creative way. Creativity is the quality that you bring to the activity you are doing. It is an attitude, an inner approach—how you look at things.

So the first thing to be remembered: Don't confine creativity to anything in particular. A man is creative, and if he is creative, whatsoever he does, even if he walks, you can see in his walking there is creativity. Even if he sits silently and does nothing, even non-doing will be a creative act. Buddha sitting under the Bodhi Tree doing nothing is the greatest creator the world has ever known.

Once you understand it—that it is you, the person, who is creative or uncreative—then this problem disappears.

Not everybody can be a painter, and there is no need also. If everybody is a painter, the world will be very ugly; it will be difficult to live! Not everybody can be a dancer, and there is no need. But everybody can be creative.

Whatsoever you do, if you do it joyfully, if you do it lovingly, if your act of doing it is not purely economics, then it is creative. If you have something growing out of it within you, if it gives you growth, it is spiritual, it is creative, it is divine.

Love what you do. Be meditative while you are doing it, whatsoever it is, irrelevant of the fact of what it is. Creativity means loving whatsoever you do—enjoying, celebrating it as a gift of existence. Maybe nobody comes to know about it, so if you are looking for fame and then you think you are creative—if you become famous like Picasso, then you are creative—then you will miss. Then you are, in fact, not creative at all; you are a politician, ambitious. If fame happens, good. If it doesn't happen, good. It should not be the consideration. The consideration should be that you are enjoying whatsoever you are doing. It is your love affair.

If your act is your love affair, then it becomes creative. Small things become great by the touch of love and delight.

The questioner asks: "I believed I was uncreative." This has been taught to everybody. Very few people are accepted as creative: a few painters, a few poets, one in a million. This is foolish. Every human being is a born creator. Watch children and you will see: all children are creative. By and by, we destroy their creativity. By and by, we force wrong beliefs on them. By and by, we distract them. By and by, we make them more and more economical and political and ambitious.

When ambition enters, creativity disappears—because an ambitious man cannot be creative, because an ambitious man cannot love any activity for its own sake. We destroy creativity. Nobody is born uncreative, but we make ninety-nine percent of people uncreative.

But just throwing the responsibility on society is not going to help. You have to take your life in your own hands. You have to drop wrong conditionings. You have to drop wrong, hypnotic auto-suggestions that have been given to you in your childhood.

A creative person comes into the world, enhances the beauty of the world—a song here, a painting there. He makes the world dance better, enjoy better, love better, meditate better. When he leaves this world, he leaves a better world behind him. Nobody may know him, somebody may know him; that is not the point. But he leaves the world a better world, tremendously fulfilled because his life has been of some intrinsic value.

If you can smile wholeheartedly, hold somebody's hand and smile, then it is a creative act, a great creative act. Just embrace somebody to your heart and you are creative. Just look with loving eyes at somebody; just a loving look can change the whole world of a person.

You are not here accidentally, you are here meaningfully. There is a purpose behind you. The whole intends to do something through you.

THE MEDITATION:
FROM GIBBERISH TO SILENCE

Today's meditation is a device to leave the mind more pure and fresh; it is one of the simplest and most scientific ways to cleanse and refresh the mind.

Osho says, "Imagine saying everything that you ever wanted to say and have not been able to say because of civilization, education, culture, society. And then saying it in any language that you have heard but you don't know! For example, if you have heard Chinese but don't know Chinese, say it in Chinese! Shouting, laughing, crying, and making noise, making gestures. Simply allow whatever comes to your mind without bothering about its rationality, reasonability, meaning, significance, just the way the birds are doing.

"Saying anything that is moving in your mind, all kinds of rubbish—throwing it out. Do it totally, with great enthusiasm."

The Technique

You can choose any time and place where you will have privacy to do the meditation, with each stage lasting five minutes. If the laughter and crying is difficult for you, you can experiment just with the first and last stage. At some point the second and third stages might arise spontaneously and be easier.

FIRST STAGE: Gibberish. Make nonsense sounds and speak any language you don't know. It is good to use the structure and the sound of human language—not just to grunt and growl and make animal noises, which has a different effect. That said, you also have total freedom to shout, scream, and express your feelings.

SECOND STAGE: Laugh. Laugh totally, for no reason at all.

THIRD STAGE: Cry and weep without any reason, to your heart's content.

LAST STAGE: Lie down—be still and silent as if you are dead, only the breathing comes and goes.

Quote of the Day

A creative act enhances the beauty of the world.
It gives something to the world, it never takes
anything from it.

—Osho

Notes

DAY 11 EVERYBODY IS CREATIVE

DAY 12

Intuition—Tuition from Within

Intuition arises in the space between the intellectual, logical mind and the more encompassing realm of spirit. Logic is how the mind knows reality; intuition is how the spirit experiences reality. Osho's discussion of these matters is wonderfully lucid, occasionally funny, and thoroughly engrossing. All people have a natural capacity for intuition, but often social conditioning and formal education work against it. People are taught to ignore their instincts, "gut feelings," and hunches, rather than to understand and use them as a foundation for individual growth and development—and in the process, the very roots of the innate wisdom that is meant to flower into intuition are undermined. Here, Osho talks about what intuition is and gives guidelines for how to distinguish between genuine intuitive insight and the "wishful thinking" that can often lead to mistaken choices and unwanted consequences.

The meditation that follows is a technique to discover the space of what is often called the witness, which is where real intuition comes from.

OSHO'S INSIGHT

There is a phenomenon called intuition of which we have become almost unaware. We don't know that anything like intuition exists.

Intuition is a totally different kind of phenomenon from reason. Reason argues; reason uses a process to reach a conclusion. Intuition jumps—it is a quantum leap. It knows no process. It simply reaches to the conclusion without any process.

There have been many mathematicians who could do any kind of mathematical problem without going into its process. Their functioning was intuitive.

Mathematicians have always been puzzled by these freak phenomena. These people—how do they do it? If a mathematician were going to do this problem it might take three hours or two hours or one hour. Even a computer will take at least a few minutes to do it, but these people don't take a single moment. You say it, and instantly. . . .

So in mathematics, intuition is now a recognized fact. When reason fails, only intuition can work. And all the great scientists have become aware of it: that all their great discoveries are made not by reason but by intuition.

Madame Curie was working for three years upon a certain problem and was trying to solve it from many directions. Every direction failed. One night, utterly exhausted, she went to sleep, and she decided. . . . The incident is almost like Buddha. That night she decided, "Now it is enough. I have wasted three years. It seems to be a futile search. I have to drop it." That night she dropped it, and went to sleep.

In the night she got up in her sleep, she went to her table and wrote the answer. Then she went back, and fell into sleep. In the morning she could not even remember, but the answer was there on the table. And there was nobody in the room, and even if there had been somebody, the answer would not have been possible. She had been working for three years—one of the greatest minds of this age. But there was nobody and the answer was there. Then she looked more minutely: it was her handwriting! Then suddenly the dream surfaced. She remembered it as if she had seen a dream in the night in which she was sitting at the table and writing something. Then by and by everything surfaced. She had come to the conclusion from some other door which was not reason. It was intuition.

But first the reason had to be exhausted. Intuition functions only when reason is exhausted. Intuition has no process; it simply jumps from the problem to the conclusion. It is a shortcut. It is a flash.

We have corrupted intuition. Man's intuition is almost absolutely corrupted. Woman's intuition is not corrupted as much—that's why women have something called a "hunch." A hunch is just a fragment of intuition. Now the woman cannot say how she knows. There is no way. It is just a hunch, just a feeling in the guts. But that too is very corrupted, that's why it is just a flash. When you have dropped fixed ideas—because you have been taught that reason is the only door to reach to any conclusion—when you have dropped this fixation, this reason fixation, intuition starts flowering. Then it is not just like a flash, it is a constantly available source. You can close your eyes and you can go into it and always you can get the right direction from it.

That's what Fischer-Hoffman people [proponents of a highly structured, time-limited, intensive psychotherapy] think of as the guide. If the process really goes in. . . . It is very difficult, because those five layers have to be crossed first. And I don't think many people are capable of it, even those who are in Fisher-Hoffman therapy. But the idea is perfectly right—if those five layers are broken then something arises in you which can be called the guide. You can always go into your intuition energy and you will always find the right advice. In the East that is what they have called the inner guru, your inner master. Once your intuition has started functioning, you need not go and ask any outer guru for any advice.

Intuition is to be in tune with oneself, totally in tune with oneself. And out of that tuning, solutions arise from nowhere.

THE MEDITATION:
FINDING THE WITNESS

"This technique," says Osho in his *Book of Secrets*, "is one of the very deep methods. . . . Try to understand this: *Attention between eyebrows* . . . Modern physiology, scientific research, says that between the two eyebrows is the gland which is the most mysterious part in the body. This gland, called the pineal gland, is the third eye of the Tibetans—*shivanetra*, the eye of Shiva, of Tantra. Between the two eyes there exists a nonfunctioning third eye. It is there and can function at any moment, but it is not naturally functioning. You have to do something about it to open it. It is not blind, it is simply closed. This technique is to open the third eye."

The Technique

Close your eyes and focus both your eyes just in the middle of the two eyebrows. It is as if you are looking with both your eyes. Give your total attention to it.

This is one of the simplest methods of being attentive. You cannot be attentive to any other part of the body so easily. This gland absorbs attention like anything; if you give attention to it, your eyes become hypnotized by the third eye. They become fixed: they cannot move. If you are trying to be attentive to any other part of the body, it is difficult. This third eye catches attention, forces attention. It is a magnet for attention. So spiritual traditions all over the world have used it. It is the simplest way to train attention, because not only are you trying to be attentive, but the gland itself helps you; it is magnetic.

Focused at the third eye, suddenly you become a witness. Through the third eye, you can see the thoughts running through your mind like clouds in the sky or like people moving on the street.

You are sitting at your window looking at the sky or at people in the street; you are not identified. You are aloof, a watcher on the hill—different. If anger is there, you can look at it as an object. Now you don't feel that *you* are angry. You feel that you are surrounded by anger—a cloud of anger has come around you—but you are not the anger. And if you are not the anger, the anger becomes impotent, it cannot affect you; you remain untouched. The anger will come and go and you will remain centered in yourself.

This can work in both directions: become a witness, and you will be centered at the third eye . . . Try to be a witness. Whatever is happening, try to be a witness to it. If you are ill, the body is aching and painful, you have misery and suffering, whatever it is: be a witness to it. Whatever is happening, don't identify yourself with it. Be a witness—an observer. Then if witnessing becomes possible, you will be focused in the third eye. The opposite is also the case: if you are focused in the third eye, you will become a witness. These two things are part of one.

Quote of the Day

Once you start living the life of truth,
authenticity, of your original face, all troubles
by and by disappear because your inner conflict
drops and you are no longer divided. Your voice
has a unity then, your whole being becomes an
orchestra.

—Osho

Notes

DAY 13

Meditation and Conditioning

In today's program, we explore the question of "conditioning" and the role it plays in our lives and who we think we are. Osho often talks about the importance of dropping the past. By this, he does not mean we need to drop the factual history of what has happened. Rather, he is talking about the imprints that the past has made on our consciousness—the programming, if you will, that all of us have been subjected to. This programming starts almost from the moment we are born. It comes from our parents, our friends, our teachers . . . the very society in which we live. Our ideas about good and bad, proper and improper, true and false, important and unimportant . . . all these things are part of our conditioning.

In the talk that follows, Osho challenges us to start becoming aware of this conditioning. To understand it and begin to be able to see it in action as we respond to situations and people around us. And, finally, to be able to free ourselves from it—to stop being what Osho calls a "humanoid," programmed by our past—and to begin the journey of discovery of the innocence and silence we were born with, what Zen people call "the original face."

OSHO'S INSIGHT

The most difficult thing in life is to drop the past—because to drop the past means to drop the whole identity, to drop the whole personality. It is to drop yourself. You are nothing but your past, you are nothing but your conditionings. And conditioning has gone very deep, because you have been conditioned from the very beginning; from the first moment you were born, conditioning started. By the time you became alert, a little aware, it had already reached the deepest core of your being. Unless you penetrate yourself to this deepest core that was not conditioned at all, that was before conditioning started, unless you become that silent and that innocent, you will never know who you are.

Meditation means to penetrate to that core, to that innermost core. Zen people call it knowing the original face.

This conditioning has to be understood first. Because of this conditioning you have lost something essential, something natural, something spontaneous in you. You are no more a human being, you only appear to be one. You have become a humanoid.

The humanoid is a being who is incapable of knowing himself, who has no idea who he is. All his ideas about himself are borrowed; they are given to him by other humanoids. The humanoid is incapable of mobilizing his own intentions; he has no more capacity to will, to be. He is a dependent phenomenon; he has lost his freedom. This, in essence, is his psychopathology.

And the whole of humanity today is psychopathological. The people who look normal to you are not normal at all. This whole earth has become a great madhouse. But because the whole earth is a madhouse, it is difficult to see. People everywhere are just like you, so you think you are normal and they are normal.

It is very rare that a normal person happens in this world—this world does not allow the normal to happen.

The humanoid is one who cannot will for himself, who is always looking for authorities, who always needs somebody else to tell him what to do.

You were born to see the truth, you were capable. Each child is able to communicate with existence, to will—but we hinder him. Parents don't allow the children to will. Then there are teachers, and those teachers are employed by the parents and the society. They are in the service of the past. The whole educational system serves the past, it does not serve you—remember it. From the kindergarten to the college, all the teachers and the professors are in the service of the past; they are there to maintain the past. They are not for you, they are not to help you; they are to condition you.

And then the priest and the politicians . . . they are all trying to condition you. Nobody wants you to be a free man, everybody wants you to be a slave, because the more you are a slave, the more easily you can be exploited. And if you follow the leaders and the priests and the pedagogues, then you have been promised all kinds of carrots; you have been promised all kinds of rewards, here and hereafter too—and now this person will remain a tyrant-needing, tyrant-seeking humanoid for the remainder of his life.

But this cannot be imposed on you. You will have to be courageous enough to drop the conditioning. Great guts will be needed.

Once you start dropping your conditionings, you will become aware of your wings. And those wings can take you to the ultimate reality: the flight of the alone to the alone. But there you can go only as an innocent being—unconditioned, utterly disidentified from the past.

That will be the first act of freedom in your life. And the first step is half the journey—the other half is very easy, it comes of its own accord.

THE MEDITATION:
THROWING THINGS OUT

Whenever you feel that the mind is not tranquil—tense, worried, chattering, anxious, constantly dreaming—do one thing: first exhale deeply. Always start by exhaling. Exhale deeply; as much as you can, throwing out the air. In doing this, the mood will be thrown out, too, because breathing is everything.

Expel the breath as far as possible. Pull the belly in and retain for a few seconds; don't inhale. Let the air be out, and don't inhale for a few seconds. Then allow the body to inhale. Inhale deeply—as much as you can. Again, stop for a few seconds. The pause should be the same as when breathing out—if you held it for three seconds, hold the breath in for three seconds. Throw it out and hold for three seconds; take it in and hold for three seconds. But the breath has to be thrown out completely. Exhale totally and inhale totally, and make a rhythm. Hold, then breathe in; hold, then breathe out. Hold, in; hold, out. Immediately you will feel a change coming into your whole being. The mood has gone; a new climate has entered you.

Quote of the Day

Society cannot tolerate individuality, because
individuality will not follow like a sheep.
The sheep are always in the crowd because
it feels more protected, secure. Only lions
move alone—and every one of you is born a
lion, but the society goes on conditioning you,
programming your mind to be a sheep.

—Osho

Notes

DAY 13 MEDITATION AND CONDITIONING

DAY 14

How to Stop Judging People

Today's Osho talk helps us to understand that it is most important to see *why* you judge and *how* you judge.

In the present moment, if you are there without thinking, just facing something like a mirror, it is witnessing—a passive awareness where no judgment is possible, because judgment can exist only against past experiences and past evaluations. It stems out of one's beliefs, ideologies, and concepts.

Thinking is possible only if the past is there, brought into the present. It is an active state in which you are *doing* something.

We are reminded that witnessing, as a passive awareness, does not mean judgment. You are not to judge that "this is good and this is bad," because the moment you judge, you're no longer witnessing. If you say "this is good," or "this is bad," you have already slipped out of witnessing and you have become a judge.

Also keep in mind that not only is every word a judgment, but language itself is burdened with judgment and can never be impartial. The moment we use a word, we have judged and created a barrier to an open mind.

In the meditation for today, we'll discover how to make judgments disappear with a simple breathing technique!

OSHO'S INSIGHT

How to drop judging people?

There is no need to stop or drop judging people; you have to understand why you judge and how you judge.

You can judge only the behavior, because only the behavior is available. You cannot judge the person because the person is hiding behind, the person is a mystery. You can judge the act, but you cannot judge the being.

And the act is irrelevant. It will not be right to judge a being through the act. Sometimes it happens that a man is smiling. The act is there on the surface, and deep inside he may be sad. In fact, he may be smiling because he is sad. He does not want to show his sadness to anybody—why bring one's wounds to everybody? Why? That seems embarrassing. Maybe he is smiling just because he is crying deep down.

So the first thing to understand is that you can look only at the behavior, and the behavior does not mean much. All that is really significant is the person behind. And you don't know. Your judgments are going to be wrong. And you know it—because when people judge you by your acts, you always feel that they have judged you wrongly. You don't judge yourself by your acts, you judge yourself by your being. So everybody feels that all judgments are unjust. You feel that judgments are unjust because to you, your being is available—and the being is such a big phenomenon, and the act is so tiny and small. It does not define anything. It may be just a momentary thing.

You said something to somebody and he became angry—but don't judge him by his anger, because it may be just a momentary flash. He may be a very loving person; if you judge him by his anger, you misjudge him. And then your behavior will depend on your judgment, and you will always wait for the man to be angry, and you will always think that he is an angry man. You will avoid the person. You have missed an opportunity! Never judge anybody by their action—but that is the only thing available to you. So what to do? "Judge ye not."

By and by, become more and more aware of the privacy of

being. Every being inside his own soul is so private, there is no way to penetrate it. Even when you love, something at the deepest core remains private. That is man's dignity. That is the meaning when we say man has a soul. Soul means that which can never become public. Something of it will always remain deep, lost in some mystery.

From the outside, that's what we can judge. From the outside it is always wrong.

Seeing it again and again, understanding it again and again, penetrating it again and again, you will not need to drop judgments; they drop of their own accord.

Just watch. Whenever you judge, you are doing something foolish. It does not apply to the person at all, it can apply only to the act. And that act, too, is taken out of context because you don't know the person's whole life. It is as if you tear a page from a novel and you read it and you judge the novel by it. It is not right; it is out of context. The whole novel may be a totally different thing. You may have taken a negative part, an ugly part.

You don't know anybody's life in its totality. A man has lived for forty years before you come to meet him; those forty years of context are there. The man is going to live forty years more when you have left him. Those forty years of context are going to be there. And you saw the man, just a single instance of him, and you judged him—that is not right. That is just stupid. It will not have any relevance to the man himself.

Your judgment will show something more about you than about the man. "Judge ye not so that ye may not be judged"— that's what Jesus says. Your judgment shows something about you, nothing about the person you have judged—because his history remains unavailable to you, his being remains unavailable to you.

All contexts are lost, there is just a momentary flash—and your interpretation will be your interpretation. It will show something about you.

Seeing this, judging disappears.

THE MEDITATION:
TRANSFORMING JUDGMENTS

Osho says,

> *"Whenever you want to change a pattern of the mind that has become a long-standing habit, changing your breathing is the best thing. All habits of the mind are associated with the pattern of breathing. Change the pattern of breathing, and the mind changes immediately, instantly. Try it."*

The Technique

Whenever you see that a judgment is coming and you are getting into an old habit, immediately exhale—as if you are throwing the judgment out with the exhalation. Exhale deeply, pulling the stomach in, and as you throw out the air, feel, visualize, that the whole judgment is being thrown out.

Then take in fresh air deeply, two or three times, and just see what happens. You will feel a complete freshness; the old habit will not have been able to take possession.

So start by exhalation, not inhalation—if you want to throw something out, start by exhalation and see how immediately the mind is affected. When you want to take something in, start inhaling.

Simply do this, and immediately you will see that the mind

has moved somewhere else; a new breeze has come. You are not in the old groove, so you will not repeat the old habit. This is true for all habits. For example, if you smoke, if the urge comes to smoke and you don't want to, immediately exhale deeply and throw the urge out. Take a fresh breath in and you will see immediately that the urge has gone. This can become a very, very important tool for inner change. Just try it!

Quote of the Day

Whenever there is no conflict between you
and the whole, not even a rumor of conflict,
you are healthy. To be whole is to be healthy.
To be whole is to be holy. And what is the way
to be holy, healthy, whole? Your heart should
beat in the same rhythm as the heart of the
whole. It is a great cosmic dance. It is a great
harmony.

—Osho

Notes

DAY 14 HOW TO STOP JUDGING PEOPLE

DAY 15

The Art of Listening

Today we live in a world where most of us are overwhelmed by a constant cacophony of sound—in effect, noise pollution. Often, these sounds are so pervasive that we no longer notice them, be they from traffic or canned music in the elevator.

Osho often speaks of "listening" as opposed to simply "hearing." The latter, he points out, is physiological and passive, while real *listening* requires presence and awareness.

Today's program on the art of listening will explore this auditory dimension of meditation. Osho will speak about the art of listening, and the meditation technique will use sound as a way to become more aware.

OSHO'S INSIGHT

The object is irrelevant. Only the subjectivity is relevant. Whether listening to me, or listening to a flute player, or listening to the birds in the morning, or sitting by the side of the waterfall and listening to it, the same experience can happen. It happens not from what you listen to, it happens because you listen. Just listening gives you total silence; in deep listening you disappear. The whole art is how to listen.

Once you know how to listen, in deep receptivity, sensitivity, you are not there. The listener is not there, only listening. And when the listener is not there, there is no ego: there is no one who listens, only listening. And then it penetrates to the very core of your being.

If you listen to me with mind, you will miss. If you listen to the waterfall without mind, you will get. It is not a question of listening to me; it is a question somewhere concerned with you, with the listener. What I am saying is irrelevant; who is saying it is irrelevant. The whole thing is: are you surrounded by a deep silence? Have you become non-existent in that moment? Do you find suddenly that you are not, that you are a deep emptiness, throbbing with life, full, but empty, a tremendous silence, with not a single ripple of thought? Only then do you attain to a plane where truth can penetrate you.

So try to be a listener. Just hearing is not enough. Hear, you can; listening will need great discipline. It is the greatest discipline there is. If you listen, you are already delivered; because in that listening, suddenly you find yourself.

This looks like a paradox. You disappear, I say, and in that disappearance you find yourself. You are empty, and in that emptiness arises a fullness, a fulfillment. No thought is there. And then there is understanding. And love flows, like breathing—it goes in, it goes out, it goes in, it goes out. Then you start sharing your being with the existence that surrounds you. Then the part is no more part and separate—it throbs with the whole. You fall in line with the whole, you are no more out of step. A harmony has arisen—the celestial music, the music of the stars.

Then suddenly you are open. From every dimension God flows into you. But the whole thing is how to be so receptive and silent.

Just sit and listen to the breeze passing through the pines . . . the whole depends on your listening. The quality of your listening is the question, not what you listen to.

THE MEDITATION:
FIND YOUR CENTER IN THE MIDDLE OF SOUND

Today's meditation uses sound to become more aware of the silent and still place inside of you that is your center.

Wherever you are right now, you are surrounded by sounds. Sounds, you will find, are always present. In your workplace, on the way to work, wherever you are, you can hear sounds . . . sounds produced by nature, or by humans, or by machines.

And with sound, there is something very special—whenever there are sounds, *you are the center.* All the sounds *come to you*, from everywhere, from all directions. Wherever you are, you are always the center of sound.

The Technique

Close your eyes . . . and feel the whole universe filled with sound.

Feel as if every sound is moving toward you, and you are the center.

The universe is the circumference, the outer, and you the center, the inner, and everything is moving toward you, falling toward you . . . as in the continuous sound of a waterfall.

When you are sitting by the side of a waterfall, you can close your eyes and feel the sound all around you, falling on you from every side, creating a center in you from every side. Or do it in a market—there is no other place like a market, it is so filled with sounds, crazy sounds.

Do not start *thinking about* sounds—that "this is good and that is bad, and this is disturbing and that is very beautiful and harmonious." Instead, stay in touch with *the center.* Don't think about the sound moving toward you, whether it is good, bad, beautiful.

Just remember that you are the center, and all the sounds are moving toward you—every sound, whatever it is.

Relax and let everything enter you. You have become more relaxed, more soft, more open . . .

Now move with the sounds, and let your attention come to the center where you hear them.

If you can feel a center where every sound is being heard, there is a sudden transference of consciousness. One moment you will be hearing the whole world filled with sounds, and in the next moment your awareness will suddenly turn in, and you will hear the soundlessness, the center of life.

Once you have heard soundlessness, then no sound can disturb you. It comes to you, but it never reaches you. It is always coming to you, but it never reaches you.

There is a point where no sound enters.

That point is you.

Once you've had a small taste of this technique, you can do it on your own, whenever you like.

Quote of the Day

There is no need to create cathedrals and great
temples—those who have eyes will find this
vast starry sky, this beautiful earth, the greatest
temple. This whole existence is a holy place.

—Osho

Notes

DAY 16

Relaxation Through Awareness

One of the key words in Osho's proposal is *understanding*. While we try to relax by watching TV, having a drink, or going on vacation, in today's excerpt, Osho helps us instead to understand how we create our tensions and anxieties in the first place.

Why don't we have control over our own bodies and minds, and why can't we just relax without all the external props? Osho takes us step by step through an understanding of how relaxation works from the outside in.

The meditation for today shows us how to set aside the need for control—one of the main drivers of tension—and allow ourselves to "let go."

OSHO'S INSIGHT

Will you say something more about relaxation? I am aware of a tension deep at the core of me and suspect that I have probably never been totally relaxed.

Total relaxation is the ultimate.

You cannot be totally relaxed right now. At the innermost core a tension will persist.

But start relaxing. Start from the circumference—that's where we are, and we can start only from where we are. Relax the circumference of your being—relax your body, relax your behavior, relax your acts. Walk in a relaxed way, eat in a relaxed way, talk, listen in a relaxed way. Slow down every process. Don't be in a hurry and don't be in haste. Move as if all eternity is available to you.

In fact, there is no beginning and no end. We have always

been here and we will be here always. Forms go on changing, but not the substance; garments go on changing, but not the soul.

Tension means hurry, fear, doubt. Tension means a constant effort to protect, to be secure, to be safe. Tension means preparing for tomorrow now, or for the afterlife—afraid that you will not be able to face the reality tomorrow, so be prepared. Tension means the past that you have not really lived but only somehow bypassed; it hangs, it is a hangover, it surrounds you.

Remember one very fundamental thing about life: any experience that has not been lived will hang around you, will persist: "Finish me! Live me! Complete me!"

You will have to relax from the circumference. The first step in relaxing is the body. Remember as many times as possible to look into the body, whether you are carrying some tension in the body somewhere—in the neck, in the head, in the legs. Relax it consciously. Just go to that part of the body, close your eyes and go to that part of the body, and persuade that part, say to it lovingly "Relax."

And you will be surprised that if you just approach any part of your body lovingly, it listens, it follows you—it is your body. With closed eyes, go inside the body from the toe to the head searching for any place where there is tension. And then talk to that part as you talk to a friend; let there be a dialogue between you and your body. Tell it to relax, and tell it, "There is no fear. Don't be afraid. I am here to take care—you can relax." Slowly, slowly you will learn the knack of it. Then the body becomes relaxed.

Then take another step, a little deeper; tell the mind to relax. And if the body listens, the mind also listens, but you cannot start with the mind—you have to start from the beginning. You cannot start from the middle. Many people start with the mind and they fail; they fail because they start from the wrong place. Everything should be done in the right order.

If you become capable of relaxing the body voluntarily, then you will be able to help your mind relax voluntarily. Mind is a more complex phenomenon. Once you have become confident that the body listens to you, you will have a new trust in yourself. Now even the mind can listen to you. It will take a little longer with the mind, but it happens.

When the mind is relaxed, then start relaxing your heart, the world of your feelings, emotions—which is even more complex, more subtle. But now you will be moving with trust, with great trust in yourself. Now you will know it is possible. If it is possible with the body and possible with the mind, it is possible with the heart too. And only then, when you have gone through these three steps, can you take the fourth. Now you can go to the innermost core of your being, which is beyond body, mind, heart: the very center of your existence. And you will be able to relax it too.

And that relaxation certainly brings the greatest joy possible, the ultimate in ecstasy, acceptance. You will be full of bliss and rejoicing. Your life will have the quality of dance to it.

THE MEDITATION:
LEARNING THE ART OF LET-GO

This meditation is best done at night.

The Technique

Lying down on your bed . . . before sleep comes, start watching.

With your eyes closed, move your awareness to the soles of the feet, and slowly start to scan your body for any tension. When you feel tension, pause and wait for the body and the breath to release that tension and let go.

Continue scanning the body moving up from the feet to the thighs and then to the buttocks, letting go of any tension.

Make sure that when you come to a place of tension in the body, remain there, with your awareness, until you feel the body move into a release.

Then move your awareness to the belly and relax the belly. As you move up to the chest and shoulders, relax the chest and shoulders.

Now relax the neck. Move your awareness now to the muscles in the face and the jaw, and relax.

Now move your awareness to the hands. The hands are connected with your mind. Look for any tension in the hands and as the tension in the hands releases, the mind releases. Now feel the weight of the hands, the weight of each finger. . . .

When the body is relaxed, the mind is relaxed. The body is just an extension of the mind. In this understanding of the body-mind dynamic is the key to relaxation, to letting go.

Quote of the Day

We are given only one moment at a time, so to live rightly one needs only to know how to live rightly in the moment. One need not worry about the whole of life. If you can take care of the present moment you have taken care of your whole life; then everything will fall into line by itself.

—Osho

Notes

DAY 16 RELAXATION THROUGH AWARENESS

_____
_____
_____
_____
_____
_____
_____
_____
_____
_____
_____
_____
_____
_____
_____
_____
_____
_____
_____
_____
_____
_____
_____
_____
_____
_____
_____
_____
_____

DAY 17

Accepting Every Part of Me

Today's program is about the disservice we do to ourselves when we judge our feelings, thoughts, and actions, fragmenting ourselves into many parts—some of which we think of as desirable, others we categorize as "bad" or in need of improvement.

Osho points out that we can accept and integrate all these parts: the good and the bad, the light and the dark, the high and the low.

In today's meditation we'll teach ourselves to see "what is" in a different way, practicing by looking at outer objects with a different quality and a never before seen "totality."

OSHO'S INSIGHT

Can you tell me about acceptance—how to learn to accept? I feel a part in me doesn't want to accept. I would like to know who that part of me is that is so stupid. Is there a way to make that part of me clearer to myself?

The first thing is to understand what acceptance means. You say: "Can you tell me about acceptance—how to learn to accept? I feel a part in me that doesn't want to accept." Accept that part also, otherwise you have not understood. A part in you goes on rejecting. Accept that rejecting part also, otherwise you have not understood. Don't try to reject that part, accept it. It is what total acceptance is. You have to also accept the part which rejects.

You say, "I would like to know who that part of me is that is so stupid." The moment you call it stupid, you have rejected it. Why do you call it stupid? Who are you to call it stupid? It is your part—why are you dividing yourself into two? You are a whole. All these tricks you have learned about division have to be dropped. You have learned to divide yourself into the godly part and the devilish part, the good and the bad, the high and the low.

Drop all divisions. That's what acceptance means. If you have something, you have something—why call it stupid? Who are you to call it stupid? No, in the very calling it stupid you have rejected it, you have condemned it.

Acceptance means there is no question of condemnation, and whatever is the case, you accept it. Suddenly, there comes a transformation in your being. Don't call it stupid, don't call it names, and don't divide yourself, because this is how the ego exists. It is the ego that is saying the other part is stupid. The ego is always intelligent, understanding, great—and it goes on rejecting. The ego teaches you to reject the body, because the body is material and you are spiritual; it teaches you to reject this and that.

All this has been done for centuries. Religious people have been doing it continuously, and they have not reached anywhere. In fact, they have made the whole of humanity schizophrenic. They have completely divided everybody into parts. You have compartments within you: this is "good" and that is "bad"; love is good, and hate is bad; compassion is good, and anger is bad.

When I say accept, I say accept all and drop all the compartments. Become one, and everything is good. Anger also has its part to play, and hate is needed too. In fact, whatever you have, everything is needed—maybe in a different arrangement, that's all. But nothing is to be denied or rejected, and don't call anything in yourself stupid.

You ask: "Is there a way to make that part of me clearer to myself?" Why? Can't you accept something hidden within yourself? Can't you accept something dark within yourself? You are also like day and night: something is in the light, something is in the dark. It has to be so, otherwise you will be just on the surface and you will not have any depth.

The depth has to be in darkness. If a tree says, "I would like to bring my roots to my knowledge," the tree dies—because roots exist only in deep darkness, hidden in the earth. There is no need to bring them up. If you bring them up, the tree will die. You need a dark part as much as you need a light part.

Don't say "stupid" to any part of yourself.

Don't fight. Allow things. That's what acceptance is—it is let-go. You live as if you are completely retired. You live, you do, but you do things naturally, spontaneously. They happen. If you feel like doing, you do; if you don't feel like doing, you don't do. By and by, you fall in line with nature, you become more and more natural.

THE MEDITATION:
LOOK AT AN OBJECT AS A WHOLE

Ordinarily, we look at parts, and we label those parts, judge them. If we look at a person, for example, we might notice the face first, then the hair, or the torso. This person is "skinny," that person is "fat." The face might strike us as warm and welcoming, angry, or cold.

This meditation is taken from an ancient text known as the *Vigyan Bhairav Tantra* and is described in detail in Osho's *Book of Secrets*. It is designed to help us step out of our habit of dividing and labeling objects and people, and to experience both ourselves and others in our pure form, which is always whole.

The Technique

THE FIRST STEP: Look upon a bowl without seeing the sides or the material.

The technique suggests a bowl, but really any object will do. The point is to find the knack of looking with a different quality.

Try it. First look at an object, such as a bowl, moving from one fragment to another. Then suddenly look at this object as a whole; do not divide it. The first thing you will discover is that when you look at an object as a whole, the eyes have no need to move. And the second part of the instruction is to look "without seeing the material." If a bowl is made of wood, don't categorize and label the wood. Just observe the bowl, the object, the form; do not think about the substance.

Why? Because substance is the material part, form is the spiritual part, and the technique is to help you move from the material to the nonmaterial. The object may be of gold, it may be of silver—just observe it. A form is just a form; you cannot think about it. If it is made of gold, you can think many things. It is beautiful, someone might want to steal it. Or if you need money you could sell it, and then you start thinking about the price—so many things are possible.

You can try it with any object, and when you start to get the knack you can even try with a person. Some man or some woman is standing there: look, and take the man or woman wholly into your look, totally into it. It will be a weird feeling in the beginning because you are not accustomed to seeing others in this way. Don't think about whether the body is beautiful or not, white or black, man or woman. Do not think; just look at the form. Forget the substance, and just look at the form.

THE SECOND STEP: *In a few moments become aware.*

Go on looking at the form as a whole. Do not allow the eyes any movement. Do not start thinking about the material it is made of, or the individual parts. What will happen? You will suddenly become aware of your self. Looking at something, you will become aware of your self. Why? Because for the eyes there is no possibility to move outward. The form has been taken as a whole, so you cannot move to the parts. The material has been dropped; pure form has been taken in. And there is no possibility of changing from one part to another; you have taken it as a whole. A form is pure form. No thinking about it is possible.

Remain with the whole and the form. Suddenly you will become aware of your self, because now the eyes cannot move. They need movement; that is their nature. So your look will move toward you. It will come back, it will return home, and suddenly you will become aware of your self. This becoming aware of one's self is one of the most ecstatic moments possible. When for the first time you become aware of your self, it has such beauty and such bliss that you cannot compare it with anything else you have known. Really, for the first time you *become* your self; for the first time you know you *are*. Your being is revealed in a flash.

Quote of the Day

Trust does not mean that everything will be
all right. Trust means everything is already
all right. Trust knows no future; trust knows
only the present. The moment you think of the
future, it is already distrust.

—Osho

Notes

DAY 17 ACCEPTING EVERY PART OF ME

DAY 18

Sex, Love, and Meditation

Osho says that sex is a simple, biological phenomenon and should not be given so much importance, that its only significance is as an energy, that it can be transformed into higher planes to become spiritual. The way to make it more spiritual, he says, is to make it a less serious affair.

Sex is a subtle and complex subject, and the very word is loaded due to our religious and cultural conditioning. Yet life itself is born out of sex. It permeates every aspect of our lives.

Osho has said, "Unless you become attuned with something beyond mind, sex is going to remain there in some form or other. And if it is going to remain there, it is better that it remains natural, biological . . .

"Lust is the lowest form of sex energy; love, the highest form. Unless your lust becomes love, you will be missing your goal . . .

"Sex is beautiful. Sex in itself is a natural, rhythmic phenomenon. Life exists through sex; sex is its medium. If you understand life, if you love life, you will know sex is sacred, holy. Then you live it, then you delight in it; and as naturally as it has come, it goes, of its own accord."

OSHO'S INSIGHT

Man has three layers: the body, the mind, and the soul. So whatsoever you do, you can do in three ways. Either it can be just from the body, or it can be from the mind, or it can be from the soul. Whatsoever you do, any act of yours, can have three qualities. Sex is love through the body; romantic love is sex through the mind; compassion is through the soul. But the energy is the same.

Moving in a deeper way, its quality changes, but the energy is the same.

If you live your love life only through the body, you live a very poor love life, because you live very superficially. Sex, just of the body, is not even sex—it becomes sexuality. It becomes pornographic, it becomes a little obscene, it becomes a little brutal, ugly, because it has no depth in it. Then it is just a physical release of the energy. Maybe it helps you to become a little less tense, but just to become a little more relaxed you are losing tremendous energy, tremendously valuable energy.

If it can become love, you will not be losing it. In the same act you will be gaining also. On the physical level there is only loss— sex is simply a loss of energy. Sex is a safety valve in the body: when the energy is too much, and you don't know what to do with it, you throw it out. You feel relaxed because you are emptied of energy. A sort of rest comes, because the restless energy is thrown out—but you are poorer than before, you are emptier than before.

And again and again this will happen. Then your whole life will become just a routine of collecting energy by food, by breathing, by exercise, and then throwing it away. This looks absurd. First eat, breathe, exercise, create energy, and then you are worried what to do with it—then throw it. This is meaningless, absurd. So sex becomes very soon meaningless. And a person who has known only sex of the body, and has not known the deeper dimension of love, becomes mechanical. His sex is just a repetition of the same act, again and again and again.

That is what is happening in the West. People are going beyond sex—not towards love, not towards compassion, because *that* beyond is within; people are going beyond sex in a negative way. Sex is becoming absurd. They are finished with it. They are searching for something else. That's why drugs have become so important. Sex is finished—that was the oldest drug, the natural LSD. Now it is finished, and people don't know what to do now. The natural drug is no more appealing, they have had enough of it. So chemicals, LSD, marijuana, psilocybin and other things are becoming more important.

In the West it is impossible now to prevent people from drugs. Unless sex starts becoming deeper and is transformed into love, there is no way: people will have to go towards drugs, helplessly. Even if they are reluctant, they will have to go, because the old drug of sex is finished. It is not finished because it was futile; it is finished because people lived only on the superficial level. They never penetrated into the mystery of it.

At the most, people know something about what they call romantic love—that too is not love; that is repressed sex. When you don't have the possibility of making a sexual contact, that repressed energy becomes romance. Then that repressed energy starts becoming cerebral, it starts moving into the head. When sex moves from the genital organs towards the head, it becomes romance. Romantic love is not really love, it is pseudo; it is a false coin. It is again the same sex, but the opportunity was not there.

In the past ages people lived very much in the romantic love because sex was not so easy. It was very difficult, the society created so many obstacles. Sex was so difficult that people had to repress it. That repressed energy would start moving into their heads, would become poetry, painting, and romance; and they would have dreams, beautiful dreams.

In the West it has disappeared, because sex has become available. Thanks to Freud there has been a great revolution in the West. The revolution has dropped all those barriers and inhibitions and repression of sex energy. Now sex is easily available, there is no problem about it.

It is so much available, more than you need—that has created a problem. Romantic love has disappeared. Now in the West, no romantic poetry is being written. Who will write romantic poetry? Sex is so easily available in the market, who will think about it? There is no need to think about it.

Romantic love is the other side of the physical sex, the repressed side. It is not love. Both are ill. What you call sex, sexuality, and romantic love—both are ill states of affairs. When body and mind meet, there is love. Love is healthy. In sexuality, only body is there; in romantic love only head is there. Both are partial.

In love, body and mind meet: you become a unity, more of a unity. You love the person, and sex comes just as a shadow to it. It is not vice versa. You love the person so much, your energies meet with the person so deeply, you feel so good by the other's presence, the other's presence is so fulfilling—it completes you. Love comes as a shadow to it.

Sex is not the center, love is the center; sex becomes the periphery. Yes, sometimes you would like to meet on the physical plane also, but there is no hankering for it. It is not an obsession, it is just a sharing of energy. The basic thing is deep. The periphery is good. With the center, the periphery is good; without the center, it becomes sexuality. Without the periphery, if it is only in the center, it becomes romantic love. When the periphery and the center are both together, there is a togetherness of body and mind. It is not only that you desire the other's body, but you desire the other's being—then there is love. Love is healthy.

Sexuality and romantic love are ill, unhealthy. They are a sort of neurosis, because they create a split in you. Love is a harmony. It is not only the body of the other, but his very being, his very presence that is loved. You don't use the other person as a means for release. You love the person. He is not, or she is not, a means but an end unto herself or unto himself. Love is healthy.

And there is another depth still left, which I call compassion. When body, mind, and soul meet, then you have become a great unity. You have become a trinity. You have become *trimurti*. Then all that is in you, from the most superficial to the deepest depth, is in a meeting. Your soul also is part of your love. Of course, compassion is possible only through deep meditation.

Sexuality is possible without any understanding, without any meditation. Love is possible only with understanding. Compassion is possible only with understanding and meditation, understanding and awareness. Not only do you understand and respect the other person, but you have come to your deepest core of being. Seeing your own deepest core, you have become capable of seeing the deepest core in the other also. Now the other does not exist as a body or a mind; the other exists as a soul. And souls are not separate. Your soul and my soul are one.

The third stage I call holy because it consists of the whole. That is possible only if you make individual efforts. Meditation will lead you to compassion. Buddha has said: If you meditate, compassion will arise automatically.

THE MEDITATION:
TRANSFORMING SEXUAL ENERGY

Each thing has its own right time, says Osho. "Each thing has to be done in its moment. While young, don't be afraid of love. If you are afraid of love while young, in old age you will become obsessed; and then it will be difficult to move deeply in love, and the mind will be obsessed."

Also, he points out: "Sex is chemical; it releases certain hormones in your body. It gives you a certain illusory euphoria. It gives you a few moments when you feel at the top of the world."

And, he cautions, "If you remain confined to sex, then you will simply waste your energy. By and by, the energy will ooze out of you, and you will remain just a dead shell."

The Technique

When the sex desire arises, close your eyes and be meditative. Move downward to the sex center where you are feeling the thrill, the vibration, the kick. Move there and just be a silent onlooker. Witness it, don't condemn it. The moment you condemn you have gone far away from it. And don't enjoy it, because the moment you enjoy you are unconscious. Just be alert, watchful, like a lamp burning in a dark night. Just take your consciousness there, unflickering, unwavering. You see what is happening at the sex center. What is this energy?

Just watch the fact that an energy is arising near the sex center. There is a thrill—watch it. You will feel a totally new quality of energy—you will see it is rising upward. It is finding a path inside you. And the moment it starts rising upward, you will feel a coolness falling on you, a silence surrounding you, a grace, a beatitude, a benediction, a blessing all around you. It is no longer like a thorn, painful. It no longer hurts; it is very soothing, like a balm. And the more you remain aware, the higher it will go. It can even rise up to the heart, which is not very difficult—difficult, but not very difficult. If you remain alert, you will see it has come to the heart. When it comes to the heart you will know for the first time what love is.

Quote of the Day

When you are making love, is your woman
really there? Is your man really there?
Or are you just doing a ritual—something
which has to be done, a duty to be fulfilled?
If you want a harmonious relationship . . .
you will have to learn to be more meditative.
Love alone is not enough. Love alone is blind;
meditation gives it eyes. Meditation gives it
understanding. And once your love is both love
and meditation, you become fellow travelers.
Then it is no longer an ordinary relationship. . . .
Then it becomes friendliness on the path toward
discovering the mysteries of life.

—Osho

Notes

_____

_____

_____

_____

_____

_____

_____

_____

_____

_____

_____

_____

_____

_____

_____

_____

_____

_____

_____

_____

_____

_____

_____

_____

_____

_____

_____

_____

DAY 19

Living in Joy

The pursuit of happiness," Osho has said, "is a basic right as set out in the Constitution of the United States. It says that the pursuit of happiness is man's birthright. If the pursuit of happiness is the birthright of mankind, then what about unhappiness? Whose birthright is unhappiness? If you ask for happiness, you have asked for unhappiness at the same time; whether you know it or not does not matter, it is the other side of the coin."

Here, Osho speaks of a different dimension—a spiritual dimension of happiness, which he calls joy. Joy is not dependent on what's going on outside, but an inner quality to be discovered.

After today's meditation, we will experiment with a technique to consciously give space to joy, to reconnect with our inherent capacity of experiencing it. The meditation builds on the technique offered on Day 17, taking it further.

OSHO'S INSIGHT

Joy is not happiness, because happiness is always mixed with unhappiness. It is never found in purity, it is always polluted. It always has a long shadow of misery behind it. Just as day is followed by night, happiness is followed by unhappiness.

Then what is joy? Joy is a state of transcendence. One is neither happy nor unhappy, but is utterly peaceful, quiet, in absolute equilibrium; so silent and so alive that his silence is a song, and his song is nothing but his silence. Joy is forever, happiness is momentary. Happiness is caused by the outside, hence can be taken away from the outside. You have to depend on others for happiness, and any dependence is ugly, any dependence is bondage.

Joy arises within; it has nothing to do with the outside. It is not caused by others. It is not caused at all, it is the spontaneous flow of your own energy.

If your energy is stagnant, there is no joy. If your energy becomes a flow, a movement, a river, there is great joy—for no other reason, just because you become more fluid, more flowing, more alive. A song is born in your heart, a great ecstasy arises.

It is a surprise when it arises, because you cannot find any cause for it. It is the most mysterious experience in life: something uncaused, something beyond the law of cause and effect. It need not be caused because it is your intrinsic nature, you are born with it. It is something inborn, it is you in your totality, flowing.

Whenever you are flowing, you are flowing towards the ocean. That is the joy: the dance of the river moving towards the ocean to meet the ultimate beloved. When your life is a stagnant pool you are simply dying. You are not moving anywhere—no ocean, no hope. But when you are flowing, the ocean is coming closer every moment, and the closer the river comes, the more dance there is, the more ecstasy there is.

Live in joy . . . Live in your own innermost nature, with absolute acceptance of whosoever you are. Don't try to manipulate yourself according to others' ideas. Just be yourself, your authentic nature, and joy is bound to arise; it wells up within you.

Live in joy, in love . . . One who lives in joy naturally lives in love. Love is the fragrance of the flower of joy.

THE MEDITATION:
MAKE ROOM FOR JOY

To know oneself is very elementary. It is not difficult, it can't be difficult; you have just to unlearn some things. You need not learn anything to know who you are, you have only to *unlearn* a few things.

First, you have to unlearn being concerned with things.

Second, you have to unlearn being concerned with thoughts.

The third thing happens of its own accord—witnessing.

The Technique

THE FIRST STAGE: First, start watching things. Sitting silently, look at a tree and just be watchful. Don't think about it. Don't say, "What kind of tree is this?" Don't say whether it is beautiful or ugly. Don't say it is "green" or "dry." Don't make any thoughts ripple around it; just go on looking at the tree.

You can do it anywhere, watching anything. Just remember one thing: when the thought comes, put it aside. Shove it aside; again go on looking at the thing.

In the beginning it will be difficult, but after a period, intervals start happening where there is no thought. You will find great joy arising out of that simple experience. Nothing has happened, it is just that thoughts are not there. The tree is there, you are there, and between the two there is space. The space is not cluttered with thoughts. Suddenly there is great joy for no visible reason, for no reason at all. Joy is a function of thoughtlessness. Joy is already there; it is repressed behind so many thoughts. When thoughts are not there, it surfaces.

You have learned the first secret.

THE SECOND STAGE: Now close your eyes and look at any thought that comes by—without thinking about the thought. Some face arises on the screen of your mind or a cloud moves, or anything; just look at it without thinking.

This process will be a little harder than the first because

thoughts are very subtle. But if the first has happened, the second will happen; only time is needed. Go on looking at the thought. After a while. . . . It can happen within weeks, it can happen within months or it can take years—it depends on how intently, how wholeheartedly you are doing it. Then one day, suddenly, the thought is not there.

You are alone. Great joy will arise—a thousandfold greater than the first joy that happened when the tree was there and the thought had disappeared. A thousandfold! It will be so immense that you will be flooded with joy.

THE THIRD STAGE: Once this has started happening, it's now time to watch the watcher. Now there is no object. Things have been dropped, thoughts have been dropped; now you are alone. Now simply be watchful of this watcher, be a witness to this witnessing.

In the beginning it will, again, be difficult because we know only how to watch *something*—a thing or a thought. But now, only the watcher is left. You have to turn upon yourself.

This is the secret key. Rest in this aloneness, and a moment comes when it happens. It is bound to happen. If the first two things have happened, the third is bound to happen; you need not worry about it.

When this happens, then for the first time you know what joy is. It is not something happening to you, so it cannot be taken away. It is you in your authentic being, it is your very being. Now it cannot be taken away. Now there is no way to lose it. You have come home.

Quote of the Day

Life is more beautiful with a little madness in it.
So never be absolutely wise. A little foolishness
gives salt to wisdom. A little foolishness gives
humor, humbleness. A really wise person is also
a fool.

—Osho

Notes

DAY 20

Maturity and the Responsibility of Being Oneself

In a culture infatuated with youth and determined to avoid old age at all costs, Osho dares to raise a question that has been all but forgotten in the age of Viagra and cosmetic surgery: What benefits might lie in accepting the aging process as natural, rather than trying to hold on to youth and its pleasures all the way to the grave?

He takes us back to the roots of what it means to grow up rather than just to grow old. Both in our relationships with others, and in the fulfillment of our own individual destinies, he reminds us of the pleasures that only true maturity can bring.

Today's meditation is called "Complete the Day."

We'll take a half hour at night and look back at our day, finishing everything that has remained incomplete.

OSHO'S INSIGHT

What is the meaning of maturity?

Maturity means the same as innocence, only with one difference: it is innocence reclaimed, it is innocence recaptured. Every child is born innocent, but every society corrupts him. Every society, up to now, has been a corruptive influence on every child. All cultures have depended on exploiting the innocence of the child, on exploiting the child, on making him a slave, on conditioning him for their own purposes, for their own ends—political, social, ideological. Their whole effort has been how to recruit the child as a slave for some purpose. Those purposes are decided by the vested interests. The priests and the politicians have been in a deep conspiracy, they both have been together.

The moment the child starts becoming part of your society

he starts losing something immensely valuable; he becomes more and more hung up in the head. He forgets all about the heart. And the heart is the bridge which leads to being; without the heart you cannot reach your own being, it is impossible. From the head there is no way directly to being; you have to go via the heart. And all societies are destructive to the heart; they are against love, they are against feelings. They condemn feelings as sentimentality. They condemned all lovers down the ages for the simple reason that love is not of the head, it is of the heart. And a man who is capable of love is sooner or later going to discover his being. And once a person discovers his being he is free from all structures, from all patterns. He is free from all bondage. He is pure freedom.

Maturity means gaining your lost innocence again, reclaiming your paradise, becoming a child again. Of course it has a difference, because the ordinary child is bound to be corrupted, but when you reclaim your childhood you become incorruptible. Nobody can corrupt you, you become intelligent enough. Now you know what the society has done to you and you are alert and aware, and you will not allow it to happen again.

Maturity is a rebirth, a spiritual birth. You are born anew, you are a child again. With fresh eyes you start looking at existence. With love in the heart you approach life. With silence and innocence you penetrate your own innermost core. You are no more just the head. Now you use the head, but it is your servant. First you become the heart, and then you transcend even the heart. . . .

Going beyond thoughts and feelings and becoming a pure is-ness is maturity. Maturity is the ultimate flowering of meditation.

To know the real beauty of your childhood, first you have to lose it; otherwise you will never know it.

The fish never knows where the ocean is—unless you pull the fish out of the ocean and throw it on the sand in the burning sun;

then she knows where the ocean is. Now she longs for the ocean, she makes every effort to go back to the ocean, she jumps into the ocean. It is the same fish and yet not the same fish. It is the same ocean yet not the same ocean, because the fish has learned a new lesson. Now she is aware, now she knows, "This is the ocean and this is my life. Without it I am no more—I am part of it."

Every child has to lose his innocence and regain it. Losing is only half of the process. Many have lost it, but very few have regained it. The moment you become aware that to be a part of any society, any religion, any culture is to remain miserable, is to remain a prisoner, that very day you start dropping your chains. Maturity is coming. You are gaining your innocence again.

Maturity is living in the present, fully alert and aware of all the beauty and the splendor of existence.

THE MEDITATION:
COMPLETE THE DAY

Osho says, "There is an intrinsic mechanism in each and every thing that compels it to become complete. A seed wants to become the tree, a child wants to become a young man, the unripe fruit wants to become ripe, and so on and so forth. Every thing wants to complete itself: it has an inbuilt urge to complete. And that is so about every experience. Every night before you go to sleep, finish that day. It is finished in existence; now it is futile to carry it in the mind. Just be finished with it. Say good-bye to it . . .

"Let there be half an hour every night, and that will be your meditation: go on finishing. Start from the morning and finish everything that has remained incomplete. You will be surprised that it can be completed. And once it has been completed you will fall into sleep."

The Technique

If something has remained incomplete in the day, complete it in the mind. You were walking down the road and you saw a person who looked so sad and distressed, and you wanted to hug that person. That cannot be done with strangers, so of course you didn't do it; now something hangs incomplete. Before you go to sleep, take thirty minutes and look back at the whole day, seeing what is incomplete. Complete those moments psychologically—hug the person, hold her hand, let her know you understand. Or, somebody insulted you, was disrespectful, and you felt like hitting them but it was not possible. It would have cost too much, and you were not ready to lose that much. Do it before you go to sleep. Relive any moment that feels incomplete instead of carrying it as incomplete.

You can always experiment with this meditation whenever you'd like.

Quote of the Day

Do anything totally and it is finished; you
will not carry a psychological memory of it.
Do anything incompletely and it hangs with
you, it goes on—it is a hangover. The mind
wants to continue and do it and complete it.
Mind has a great temptation to complete things.
Complete anything and the mind has gone.
If you continue doing things totally, one day you
suddenly find there is no mind. The mind is the
accumulated past of all incomplete actions.

—Osho

Notes

DAY 21

Zorba the Buddha

Today we introduce you to "Zorba the Buddha," Osho's vision of a new human being who is whole, not split between materialism and spirituality—a person able to celebrate every aspect of life.

One dimension of the new man is represented by Zorba the Greek, as described in Nikos Kazantzakis's novel *Zorba the Greek* and made famous by Anthony Quinn in a movie of the same name. Zorba is a man who embraces the pleasures of the body through all his senses. He enjoys life to the fullest. Zorba is playfulness.

The other dimension of the new man is represented by Buddha, the embodiment of the spiritual, the silence and awareness that lie beyond the material world, or hidden in its deepest depths.

For Osho, these two are complementary, not in opposition, and he points out that the division of these two parts of who we are has driven humanity to the point of insanity. Osho's vision is the synthesis of Zorba and Buddha: "Zorba the Buddha."

Our meditation today will give you a taste of what happens when Zorba and Buddha are one. It enhances the pleasure of the senses while giving you an experience of silent awareness at the same time.

OSHO'S INSIGHT

Sometimes when you speak, I get the vision of living a kind of Zorba the Greek life—eat, drink and be merry—lusty and passionate, and I think this is the way. Other times I feel you are saying that the way is to sit silently, watchful and unmoving, like a monk. I sense that you have managed to integrate the contradictions, but can we be both Zorbas, moved by passion and desire, and Buddhas, dispassionate, cool and calm?

That is the ultimate synthesis—when Zorba becomes a buddha. I am trying to create here not Zorba the Greek but Zorba the Buddha.

Zorba is beautiful, but something is missing. The earth is his, but the heaven is missing. He is earthly, rooted, like a giant cedar, but he has no wings. He cannot fly into the sky. He has roots but no wings.

Eat, drink and be merry is perfectly good in itself: nothing is wrong in it. But it is not enough. Soon you will get tired of it. One cannot just go on eating, drinking and merrying. Soon the merry-go-round turns into a sorry-go-round—because it is repetitive. Only a very mediocre mind can go on being happy with it. If you have a little intelligence, sooner or later you will find the utter futility of it all. How long can you go on eating, drinking and merrying? Sooner or later the question is bound to arise—what is the point of it all? Why? It is impossible to avoid the question for long. And if you are very intelligent, it is always there, persistently there, hammering on your heart for the answer: "Give me the answer!—*why*?"

And one thing to be remembered: it is not that the people who are poor, starving, become frustrated with life—no. They cannot become frustrated. They have not lived yet—how can they be frustrated? They have hopes. A poor man always has hopes. A poor man always desires that something is going to happen, hopes that something is going to happen. If not today then tomorrow, or the day after tomorrow. If not in this life then in the next life.

What do you think? Who are these people who have depicted heaven as a Playboy Club—who are these people? Starved, poor, who have missed their life. They are projecting their desires in heaven. In heaven there are rivers of wine.

Starved, have not been able to live their life. How can they be frustrated with life? They have not experienced—it is only through experience that one comes to know the utter futility of it all. Only Zorbas come to know the utter futility of it all.

Buddha himself was a Zorba. He had all the beautiful women available in his country. His father had arranged for all the beautiful girls to be around him. He had the most beautiful palaces—different places for different seasons. He had all the luxury that is possible, or that was possible in those days. He lived the life of a Zorba the Greek—hence, when he was only twenty-nine he became utterly frustrated. He was a very intelligent man. If he had been a mediocre man, then he would have lived in it. But soon he saw the point: it is repetitive, it is the same. Every day you eat, every day you make love to a woman . . . and he had new women every day to make love to. But how long . . . ?! Soon he was fed up.

The experience of life is very bitter. It is sweet only in imagination. In its reality it is very bitter. He escaped from the palace and the women and the riches and the luxury and everything. . . .

So, I am not against Zorba the Greek because Zorba the Greek is the very foundation of Zorba the Buddha. Buddha arises out of that experience. So I am all for this world, because I know the other world can only be experienced through this world. So I don't say escape from it, I will not say to you become a monk. A monk is one who has moved against the Zorba; he is an escapist, a coward; he has done something in a hurry, out of unintelligence. He is not a mature person. A monk is immature, greedy—greedy for the other world, and wants it too early, and the season has not come, and he is not ripe yet.

Live in this world because this world gives a ripening, maturity, integrity. The challenges of this world give you a centering, an awareness. And that awareness becomes the ladder. Then you can move from Zorba to Buddha.

But let me repeat again: only Zorbas become buddhas—and Buddha was never a monk. A monk is one who has never been a Zorba and has become enchanted by the words of buddhas. A monk is an imitator, he is false, pseudo. He imitates buddhas. He may be Christian, he may be Buddhist, he may be a Jaina—that doesn't make much difference—but he imitates buddhas.

You can get into the higher only when you have lived through the lower. You can earn the higher only by going through all the agony and the ecstasy of the lower. Before a lotus becomes a lotus it has to move through the mud—that mud is the world. The monk has escaped from the mud, he will never become a lotus. It is as if a lotus seed is afraid of falling into mud—maybe out of ego that "I am a lotus seed! And I cannot fall into the mud." But then it is going to remain a seed; it will never bloom as a lotus.

I would like you to become rooted into the earth. Don't hanker for the other world. Live this world, and live it with intensity, with passion. Live it with totality, with your whole being. And out of that whole trust, out of that life of passion, love and joy, you will become able to go beyond.

The other world is hidden in this world. The Buddha is asleep in the Zorba. It has to be awakened. And nobody can awaken you except life itself.

I am here to help you to be total wherever you are, in whatsoever state you are—live that state totally. It is only living a thing totally that one transcends it.

First become a Zorba, a flower of this earth, and earn the capacity through it to become a buddha—the flower of the other world. The other world is not away from this world; the other world is not against this world: the other world is hidden in this—this is only a manifestation of the other, and the other is the unmanifest part of it.

THE MEDITATION:

BECOME THE TASTE OF THE FOOD OR THE DRINK

When Osho talks about "experiencing the other world through this world," and says that "the other world is hidden in this world, the Buddha asleep in the Zorba" and that "the other world is not against this world, it is a manifestation of it"—how can we experience this? How do we practice healing the inner "division" between our "Zorba" and our "Buddha" so that they become one whole again?

Again, the key here has to do with "being total" in some activity in the here and now. Today's method is simple, instant, and enjoyable. You can practice it during your next meal or snack time today, if you like. Schedule a little extra time for that meal.

Read the instructions again before you do it, to refresh your memory and to help you get in the space to do it. It is easiest to practice this when you are alone—or when you agree with your friends or family to do this together for something like ten to fifteen minutes, before you then go back to normal and start up your usual mealtime talk as you like.

The Technique

Here is the method, explained in Osho's words in *The Book of Secrets*:

"When eating or drinking, become the taste of the food or drink, and be filled."

The next time you're eating or drinking, go slow, and be aware of the taste of the food. Only when you go slow can you be aware. Do not just swallow things—taste them unhurriedly and become the taste. When you feel sweetness, become that sweetness. And then it can be felt all over the body—not just in the mouth, not just on the tongue, it can be felt all over the body! A certain sweetness—or anything else—is spreading in ripples. Whatever you are eating, feel the taste and become the taste.

When drinking water, feel the coolness. Close your eyes, drink it slowly, taste it. Feel the coolness and feel that you have become that coolness, because the coolness is being transferred to you from the water; it is becoming a part of your body. Your mouth is touching, your tongue is touching, and the coolness is transferred. Allow it to happen to the whole of your body. Allow its ripples to spread, and you will feel a coolness all over your body. In this way your sensitivity can grow, and you can become more alive and more filled."

That's it! Do this as often as you like and for as long as you like. You'll get the taste of the "Zorba the Buddha" flavor of an enhanced pleasure of the senses accompanied by a silent awareness very easily, and you can play with this principle in other dimensions of your life as well.

Quote of the Day

Everybody is telling you to keep a low profile.
Why? Such a small life, why keep a low profile?
Jump as high as you can. Dance as madly as
you can.

—Osho

Notes

DAY 21 ZORBA THE BUDDHA

Recommended Reading by Topic

TOPIC	RECOMMENDED READING
DAY 1 What Is Meditation?	*Meditation: The First and Last Freedom*
DAY 2 Meditations on Love and Relating	*Being in Love: How to Love with Awareness and Relate Without Fear*
DAY 3 Meditations on Anger	*Emotional Wellness: Transforming Fear, Anger, and Jealousy into Creative Energy*
DAY 4 Living in Balance	*When the Shoe Fits: Stories of the Taoist Mystic Chuang Tzu*
DAY 5 Love and Meditation Hand in Hand	*Tantra: The Supreme Understanding*
DAY 6 Living Dangerously	*Living Dangerously: Ordinary Enlightenment for Extraordinary Times*
DAY 7 Watching the Mind	*The Book of Understanding: Creating Your Own Path to Freedom*
DAY 8 It Needs Intelligence to Be Happy	*Joy: The Happiness That Comes from Within*
DAY 9 Integration of Body, Mind, and Soul	*Body Mind Balancing*

DAY 10 Slowing Down	*The Art of Living and Dying*
DAY 11 Everybody Is Creative	*Creativity: Unleashing the Forces Within*
DAY 12 Intuition—Tuition from Within	*Intuition: Knowing Beyond Logic*
DAY 13 Meditation and Conditioning	*Meditation for Busy People*
DAY 14 How to Drop Judging People	*Words from a Man of No Words*
DAY 15 The Art of Listening	*Gold Nuggets: Messages from Existence*
DAY 16 Relaxation Through Awareness	*The Chakra Book: Energy and Healing Power of the Subtle Body*
DAY 17 Accepting Every Part of Me	*The Magic of Self-Respect*
DAY 18 Sex, Love, and Meditation	*Sex Matters: From Sex to Superconsciousness*
DAY 19 Living in Joy	*In Love with Life: Reflections on Friedrich Nietzsche's Thus Spake Zarathustra*
DAY 20 Maturity and the Responsibility of Being Oneself	*The Buddha Said . . . : Meeting the Challenge of Life's Difficulties*
DAY 21 Zorba the Buddha	*The Search: Finding Your Inner Power, Your Potential*

Osho International Meditation Resort

LOCATION

Located 100 miles southeast of Mumbai in the thriving modern city of Pune, India, the OSHO International Meditation Resort is a holiday destination with a difference. The Meditation Resort is spread over twenty-eight acres of spectacular gardens in a beautiful tree-lined residential area.

OSHO MEDITATIONS

A full daily schedule of meditations for every type of person includes both traditional and revolutionary methods, and particularly the OSHO Active Meditations®. The meditations take place in what may be the world's largest meditation hall, the OSHO Auditorium.

OSHO MULTIVERSITY

Individual sessions, courses and workshops cover everything from creative arts to holistic health, personal transformation, relationship and life transition, transforming meditation into a lifestyle for life and work, esoteric sciences, and the "Zen" approach to sports and recreation. The secret of the OSHO Multiversity's success lies in the fact that all its programs are combined with meditation, supporting the understanding that as human beings we are far more than the sum of our parts.

OSHO BASHO SPA

The luxurious Basho Spa provides for leisurely open-air swimming surrounded by trees and tropical green. The uniquely styled, spacious Jacuzzi, the saunas, gym, tennis courts . . . all these are enhanced by their stunningly beautiful setting.

CUISINE

A variety of different eating areas serve delicious Western, Asian and Indian vegetarian food—most of it organically grown especially for the Meditation Resort. Breads and cakes are baked in the resort's own bakery.

NIGHTLIFE

There are many evening events to choose from—dancing being at the top of the list! Other activities include full-moon meditations beneath the stars, variety shows, music performances and meditations for daily life.

Or you can just enjoy meeting people at the Plaza Café, or walking in the nighttime serenity of the gardens of this fairytale environment.

FACILITIES

You can buy all of your basic necessities and toiletries in the Galleria. The OSHO Multimedia Gallery sells a large range of OSHO media products. There is also a bank, a travel agency and a Cyber Café on campus. For those who enjoy shopping, Pune provides all the options, ranging from traditional and ethnic Indian products to all of the global brand-name stores.

ACCOMMODATION

You can choose to stay in the elegant rooms of the OSHO Guesthouse, or for longer stays on campus you can select one of the OSHO Living-In program packages. Additionally there is a plentiful variety of nearby hotels and serviced apartments.

www.osho.com/meditationresort

www.osho.com/guesthouse

www.osho.com/livingin

About the Author

For more information: www.OSHO.com

Osho is a comprehensive multilanguage website, including a magazine, OSHO Books, OSHO TALKS in audio and video formats, the OSHO Library text archive in English and Hindi, and extensive information about OSHO Meditations. You will also find the program schedule of the OSHO Multiversity and information about the OSHO International Meditation Resort.

Websites:

http://OSHOTIMES.com

http://OSHO.com/Resort

http://www.YouTube.com/OSHOinternational

http://www.Twitter.com/OSHO

http://www.Facebook.com/OSHO.International

http://www.Instagram.com/OSHO.International

To contact OSHO International Foundation:

www.osho.com/oshointernational

oshointernational@oshointernational.com

ABOUT OSHO

Osho defies categorization. His thousands of talks cover everything from the individual quest for meaning to the most urgent social and political issues facing society today. Osho's books are not written but are transcribed from audio and video recordings of his extemporaneous talks to international audiences. As he puts it, "So remember: whatever I am saying is not just for you . . . I am talking also for the future generations." Osho has been described by the *Sunday Times* in London as one of the 1000 Makers of the 20th Century and by American author Tom Robbins as "the most dangerous man since Jesus Christ." *Sunday Mid-Day* (India) has selected Osho as one of ten people—along with Gandhi, Nehru and Buddha—who have changed the destiny of India. About his own work, Osho has said that he is helping to create the conditions for the birth of a new kind of human being. He often characterizes this new human being as "Zorba the Buddha"–capable both of enjoying the earthy pleasures of a Zorba the Greek and the silent serenity of a Gautama the Buddha. Running like a thread through all aspects of Osho's talks and meditations is a vision that encompasses both the timeless wisdom of all ages past and the highest potential of today's (and tomorrow's) science and technology. Osho is known for his revolutionary contribution to the science of inner transformation, with an approach to meditation that acknowledges the accelerated pace of contemporary life. His unique OSHO Active Meditations are designed to first release the accumulated stresses of body and mind, so that it is then easier to take an experience of stillness and thought-free relaxation into daily life.

Two autobiographical works by the author are available:

Autobiography of a Spiritually Incorrect Mystic

Glimpses of a Golden Childhood

Also by the international bestselling author
OSHO

Available everywhere books are sold

HARMONY
BOOKS